BETWEEN
HEAVEN
AND
HEALING

"So do not fear, for I am with you; do not be dismayed for I am your God. I will strengthen you and help you; I will uphold you with my righteous right hand."

Isaiah 41:10

Melanie Boulis

BETWEEN HEAVEN AND HEALING

Accepting God's Will for Danielle:
A Mother's Journey

M E L A N I E   B O U L I S

Inspiring Voices®
A Service of **Guideposts**

ISBN: 978-1-4624-0473-5 (s)
ISBN: 978-1-4624-0474-2 (e)

Library of Congress Control Number: 2012923339

Inspiring Voices books may be ordered through booksellers or by contacting:

Inspiring Voices
1663 Liberty Drive
Bloomington, IN 47403
www.inspiringvoices.com
1-(866) 697-5313

Because of the dynamic nature of the Internet, any web addresses or links contained in this book may have changed since publication and may no longer be valid. The views expressed in this work are solely those of the author and do not necessarily reflect the views of the publisher, and the publisher hereby disclaims any responsibility for them.

Any people depicted in stock imagery provided by Thinkstock are models, and such images are being used for illustrative purposes only.

Certain stock imagery © Thinkstock.

Printed in the United States of America

Inspiring Voices rev. date: 01/03/2013

To all who prayed for our family through Danielle's illness and through grieving her death.

To those who blessed us financially and in countless other ways as you became God's hands, feet, and heart to us. May your reward in heaven be great for all that you've done for our family!

To all of the doctors, nurses and other staff who took such good care of Danielle to make her as comfortable as possible during her battle with cancer.

To my wonderfully talented cousin, Vicki Hoehner, for her invaluable input to this book and for her editing expertise.

To Carma Yoder for stepping in to "save the day" by agreeing to give this book a final edit and finishing it in record time.

THANK YOU!

Now that you're in heaven/ Tell me what you see / Is He as beautiful / As I picture Him to be / Running through the streets of gold / Dancing with the King / I guess it's selfish / To want you back with me / But I can't help but shed some tears / Wishing I could have you here with me / But I know / You see Jesus / You see Jesus / You see Jesus everywhere / You can touch Him / You can know Him / You can speak with Him face to face / Now that you're in heaven / Tell me what you see / Are you and Jesus watching over me / Do you see me struggling / Can you feel my pain / Wishing I could hold you / In my arms again / But I can almost hear your voice / Soothing me, whispers / "Rejoice, I'm with Him / And I see Jesus / I see Jesus / I see Jesus everywhere / I can touch Him / I can know Him / I can speak with Him face to face / So remember in your darkest hour / When things just don't seem fair / Don't lose sight of what He promised you / He's with you / Right by your side / Do you see Jesus / Do you see Jesus / Do you see Jesus everywhere / Can you feel Him / Do you trust Him / Don't you know He's present everywhere" / Now that you're in heaven / Tell me what you've learned / You're now a witness / Of mysteries unheard / Is it true that heaven / Begins here on earth / And we can know Him now / If we believe His word / I know someday we'll all be there / And bowing with you we'll declare / "I see Jesus / I see Jesus / I see Jesus everywhere / I can know Him / I can touch Him / I can speak with Him face to face"

"Face to Face"

Words: Stephanie Staples & Matthew Jonker
Music: Stephanie Staples
(c)2005 Face to Face ASCAP

Contents

1

Something Is Terribly Wrong

*L*IFE WAS GOOD. WE HAD a house to live in; we were finally keeping up with bills; and my two kids, Levi and Danielle, were doing well in school and both loved God. My husband, Kevin, and I were serving the Lord at a small church that we had been at a little over two years. Other than being crazy busy working full-time and volunteering for countless church ministries, I didn't have much to complain about. In hindsight, it was the calm before the storm.

Danielle, our second child, then twelve and in sixth grade, had been shooting up in height. With that came clumsiness, like her mother (I was hoping that trait would skip over her). Then there were little things, like our quiet daughter suddenly talking louder, almost blaring at times. Globs of ketchup or bits of food seemed to be always on one side of her mouth while eating. Danielle was oblivious to it being there, so we were constantly reminding her to wipe her mouth off, even suggesting that she start doing that every so often at school lunch, even if she thought there was nothing there. She had never been the neatest eater, so no big deal. We reasoned all of it away until the day we had to admit to ourselves that her walking was not normal.

Trying to make her way to Kevin's car after school, she resembled a drunken person trying to walk a straight line for the officer. Later that night, her daddy asked her to walk an imaginary tightrope line and she couldn't do it without falling. The next day we scheduled an appointment with her doctor. He referred us to a neurologist. Danielle's pediatrician said that it could be something simple or something serious, but he wasn't sure. A few days later, the neurologist in Bryan watched Danielle's eye movements, watched her walk, and asked us a series of questions. After ordering tests for the following week the neurologist sent us home to wait. The "what if's" started playing in our minds, though we didn't voice them to anyone else. We waited and prayed.

At the beginning of the week, Danielle had a specialized hearing and vision test. The second test that she had was a Magnetic Resonance Imaging (MRI) on a Thursday morning. Danielle returned to school afterward and Kevin and I back to work.

After school, Kevin and Danielle traveled to Levi's track meet. The cell phone rang.

"The MRI results for Danielle are in. Can you come this afternoon into the office to discuss the results?" the neurologist's secretary asked.

Kevin replied, "No, I am already more than half-way to an away track meet for my son. Even if I turn around now, I wouldn't be able to get to your office by closing time. Can I come in tomorrow?"

"We would like to see you as soon as possible. Tomorrow will be fine if that is the soonest you can make it."

Kevin called to tell me what the office said. I thought it would be pretty easy for me to go to the doctor's office right away, since I was just a few minutes away. I had just gotten home for my supper break from work, so I called my supervisor and said I might be a little late because I was going to get the MRI results.

2

Devastating News

$\mathcal{A}$s soon as Dr. Palichero (the neurologist) and the visiting neurosurgeon asked if I would like to sit down, I knew something wasn't right. I stayed standing, as if somehow the news would have to be good if I didn't sit down. They showed me the slides from Danielle's MRI and pointed out a large tumor on her brain stem. I immediately lowered myself into a chair, numb from shock and disbelief. My world was changed in that moment. This couldn't be happening to my baby—not the sweet, shy little girl I loved with all my being. The neurosurgeon told me that Danielle had a complicated case, and we needed to be at a children's hospital with experienced pediatric neurosurgeons. He suggested we drive to Riley Children's Hospital in Indianapolis, since that was a little closer than Cincinnati. We were to leave ASAP and drive straight to Riley, have Danielle not eat anything, and we were not to tell her what was happening. The pressure on her brain from a build-up of fluids was a worry. They didn't want her to be upset, which could aggravate the situation.

The nurse gently asked if she could call my husband for me. I thanked her, but told her I would call him myself. I didn't have a cell phone, so she let me use the office phone. By this time, it was after hours and the halls were empty. It felt like I was in a dream world. This couldn't be reality. Any moment I would wake up and return to life as normal. I called Kevin and told him that the doctors had found a large brain tumor, and he needed to leave the track meet with Danielle and come home. Thank God that he had a cell phone! He told our son, Levi, that we needed to take Danielle to the hospital and headed home.

In the meantime, I drove myself home. I only had a home phone that could make local calls, so I went over to the daycare at our church, and the ladies helped me dial out. Luckily, only one or two kids and two workers were left. Shaking, I called a lady from church to get everyone praying and called my mother-in-law to come be with Levi. She lived a little over an hour and a half away. I managed to muddle through a few more phone calls, including work, and then broke down while telling the daycare workers what was happening. They had just been cleaning up to leave. One of them asked if she could pray with me. That was the first of thousands of prayers that were prayed for Danielle's brain tumor. It was good to be hugged and have someone to cry with before I walked home to our empty house to pack bags for a hospital stay.

I was told to pack for a few days. Keeping my mind occupied until Kevin and Danielle arrived was probably a blessing. I tend to get over-emotional about everything in life.

It was almost suppertime when we left, and all three of us had the first stomach rumblings of hunger. I explained to Danielle that we had to wait to see what they would say at Riley before we could eat. Calls kept coming to our cell phone on the road trip. We had to be very vague and try not to cry on the phone. I wanted so badly to talk to my parents, but we just told everyone we would call later when we were at the hospital. At least if we were in a building, we could talk in another room out of earshot of Danielle.

The three-hour trip became four and a half hours. We were caught in a horrendous traffic jam. Tired, hungry, and stressed, we were so anxious to move! Danielle's biggest concern was for food and hopes of getting a female doctor when we got there. She asked us some questions, many of which we couldn't answer specifically. All she knew was that we were going to a hospital in Indianapolis so they could check her out. I'm sure that she was nervous, but she didn't voice that to us. She just said that she was fine and didn't understand why everyone was making a big deal about her. That was typical Danielle—not wanting to be the focus of attention. I was in the front seat, fighting back tears and praying non-stop all the way to a destination that I didn't want to be headed toward.

They were expecting us at Riley Hospital. The neurosurgeon had phoned ahead. MRI scans in hand, we helped Danielle stagger to the door of the emergency room. Dr. Kimm was working the ER that night. God knew who we needed to be on duty. Dr. Kimm was able to explain everything so completely to Danielle. He even had her laughing at one point—unbelievable! Compassionate and great with kids, he walked us through that horrific night better than I could imagine anyone else doing. The immediate goal was getting the fluid drained off the brain. The tumor was pressing on the ventricles, causing them not to drain, and the fluid build-up was causing tremendous pressure. Danielle was scheduled for the first surgery of her life that next morning to get an extraventricular drain put in.

Sleep was elusive for Kevin and me that first night in the hospital. I lay in a pullout chair and Kevin tried to sleep on the waiting room floor with a blanket and pillow. Danielle wanted to be at home in her own bed, feeling safe, secure, and normal. Sleep finally overtook hunger for her.

The next day, Danielle got to meet her neurosurgeon, Dr. Smith. From the relieved look on Danielle's face, we knew her prayer was answered for a female doctor. Dr. Smith said the tumor was quite large, about the size of a racquetball. "It is on the brain stem and against some important bundles of nerves, so it may be hard to get it all, but I'll try to get as much as I can," she said. "Today, though, we need to get that fluid build-up in your head draining."

The surgery didn't take too long, but then came the four-hour long MRI. Danielle had a hard time being still after surgery, so morphine was given. The MRI was for the brain and the whole spine. The good thing about brain tumors, we were told, is that the only area they spread might be the spine. After every procedure, Danielle kept asking if she could eat yet. She was denied food until 7:30 Friday night and hadn't eaten a meal since Thursday lunch. Talk about hungry and cranky! Thirsty too! She wasn't allowed to drink before her surgery or the MRI. After all the tests of the day, we ordered her some food, but by the time it got there she was too tired to eat much. Luckily, she was able to get a drink right away.

As we waited for Monday's surgery, I was singing the words of songs that kept running through our minds. "I will say of the Lord, he is my refuge and my fortress. My God, in Him will I trust,"(*He That Dwelleth* by John Jimenez) and, "I need you Jesus to come to my rescue. Where else can I go? There's no other name by which I am saved. Capture me with grace. I will follow you." (*Rescue* by Jared Anderson) Our wonderful friend, Toni, was praying Psalm 20 over Danielle and encouraging others to do so as well.

Psalm 20: "May the Lord answer you when you are in distress; may the name of the God of Jacob protect you. May He send you help for the sanctuary and grant you support from Zion. May he remember all your sacrifices and accept your burnt offerings. May He give you the desire of our heart and make all your plans succeed. We will shout for joy when you are victorious and will lift up our banners in the name of our God. May the Lord grant all your requests. Now I know that the Lord saves his anointed; He answers Him from His holy heaven with the saving power of his right hand. Some trust in chariots and some in horses, but we trust in the name of the Lord our God. They are brought to their knees and fall, but we rise up and stand firm. Lord, give victory to the King, answer us when we call."

The day after the extraventricular drain surgery (EVD) to begin draining the fluid build-up in her brain, Danielle was able to visit with grandparents. Child Life Staff, there to provide emotional support to the children and families, came and brought a Candy Land game to keep, movies to borrow, and crafts to keep Dani occupied. She had always loved playing games and doing crafts, so Grandma Miriam, my mom, and Dani did those things together. It was frustrating for Danielle trying to paint with being hooked up to IV's. Levi was able to join us, too. He had a way of always making Danielle laugh. Just being together as a whole family again felt as close to normal as we could get.

3

Is This a Bad Dream?

WHAT A DIFFERENT WORLD IT was in the Intensive Care Unit (ICU) of a children's hospital. Just a couple days ago, we were living life normally with school and work. Now nothing mattered except getting my little girl better. Our dog, Sampson, was being cared for by our neighbor, Dan. Grandma Ann, Kevin's mom, took care of Levi while we were in the hospital and took care of Danielle's rabbit, Spencer, and her new hermit crab, Scooter. The library could carry on without me, and the church could function without us for a time.

Kevin and I prayed and wished we could trade places with the brown-eyed, curly-haired girl in the hospital gown. We were helpless to be able to do much, but we stayed close beside our girl, prayed with her, read her Scripture, sang to her, and comforted her. We were completely reliant on God!!

We trusted Him to give wisdom and skill to the doctors and nurses.

A couple days later, surrounded by family and friends, we said good-bye to Danielle as they wheeled her off for a tumor resection (partial removal of the tumor) in the capable hands of Dr. Smith. Dr. Smith was also a praying and deeply compassionate doctor. I told the Lord, once again, that I was giving my daughter back into His hands. He gave Danielle to us, her earthly parents, but I always knew that my children were ultimately His. He created them and loves them even more than I do. His love is perfect! Even though I can't fathom how anyone could love my little girl more than I do, I know that her heavenly Father does.

After hours of waiting and praying together, we heard from the "surgery runner" that the tumor was deeper down than a typical tumor, and it was taking a long time to get to it. As soon as Dr. Smith could, she sent a specimen off to pathology.

Their initial call was that the tumor was a slow-growing, benign one. We all praised the Lord for that report. What a relief!

Finally, after a grueling thirteen-hour wait, the surgery was over. It took two hours just for the doctor to close everything up in Danielle's head. Our family and friends left to go get some sleep.

A weary Dr. Smith briefed us about how the surgery went. When she reached the tumor, she found it enmeshed with the brain stem. It was hard to separate brain stem from tumor. The tumor had "fingers" wrapping in and around the brain stem. The tumor was also quite vascular, so excessive bleeding was an issue as well. She had taken out what she safely could, trying to avoid permanent deficits. All in all, Dr. Smith seemed happy with the surgery and that she had accomplished as much as she could.

We found out that Dani was completely annoyed at the nurses when they woke her up after surgery to ask her questions and make her wiggle her toes and fingers. The nurses told us she had whined, "Leave me alone! How am I supposed to get any sleep?" After they were sure she was doing fine, they gave her morphine for the pain.

She was out cold when they called Kevin and me to come see her. She wouldn't wake up at all for us, but we talked to her in the recovery room. It was so strange to see her with her head bandaged up and her face swollen. At that moment, the reality of her situation hit me fiercely in the gut. I ached to envelop her in a bear hug, but with all the IV's, I had to settle for holding her hand. "I love you," I whispered. "Sleep well."

We got up to the ICU room at two in the morning. I eased my weary body into a chair beside Danielle in case she woke up. Kevin reluctantly headed out the door to sleep at the Ronald McDonald house.

A Computed Tomography Scan (CT scan) was scheduled for first thing in the morning, using X-rays to make a detailed picture of her brain. They found there was no hemorrhaging or excessive swelling. Later that morning, she began opening her eyes a few seconds at a time. After some morphine in the afternoon, the nurses got Danielle to move her neck with a little help. They said that this would be crucial for the healing process. She drank a little, but she wasn't alert enough to eat the Combos that she was really looking forward to eating after the surgery. The last thing she had eaten was a McFlurry from Grandpa Ralph, my dad, the evening before. He was so proud to be able to give her something that made his only granddaughter smile.

After surgery, in place of Dani's smile was a face that was contorted in agonizing pain. She was on pain meds that kept her pretty zonked out for a couple days other than when she would wake up and scream. She did not want to move her head at all! The nurses switched meds so she could be alert enough to eat something. It was encouraging to see her eating and moving her neck a little.

A few days after her tumor resection, she began asking when she could go home. The end was not in sight, so we had to be honest and tell her that we had no idea. I read the verses aloud that my friend, Toni, had given me. She had written hand-picked scriptures that she thought would be encouraging to us as I spent days and nights watching my little girl suffer. I never tired of hearing those verses. They were water to my dry, thirsty soul. (I still, to this day, pick up those index card verses and read them when I want to be assured of God and His promises but don't know which book of the Bible I want to read.) I wanted Danielle to hear of God's promises for her, too. After all, as hard as it was watching her, I'm sure it was far worse being the one lying in that hospital bed, wondering where God was in the midst of all her pain. I trust that His angels were ministering to Danielle and comforting her.

More MRI's and other scans to check her brain followed. There was now a cavity in the brain where a chunk of the tumor was taken out. The remaining part of the tumor was against the brain stem, which was bowed from the pressure. It had straightened out only slightly. The drain wasn't draining well. A benefit of the EVD was that since it was on the outside of her head, we could see the fluid going through the tube and into the measuring device. Because of the EVD, they had cautioned Dani to not sit up much unless the nurses were there to adjust it.

One day, she was having a meltdown and bolted upright in bed, which caused the EVD to begin draining rapidly. Despite Dr. Kimm coming to tell her not to do that, she repeatedly disobeyed orders. Clearly, she was not in her right mind because of pain and meds. Normally she was obedient, to a fault, to any authority. The nurses had to give Danielle morphine to calm her down and help her to sleep soundly.

4

Support From God's Family

CARDS WERE POURING IN FROM all over the U.S. and beyond. Flowers, balloons, and stuffed animals were being sent too. Many of the cards had a gift of money inside. The hospital had it set up that people could e-mail Dani from the hospital's website. She was given a print-out every day. Kevin read the e-mails to her, and I read the cards and letters. All of the encouraging words meant a lot to Kevin and me. We were totally amazed and humbled by how many were praying and overwhelmed by how the family of God was coming together in our time of need. Danielle's 6th grade class all made cards for her, as well as some kids from other classes. Her wonderful teacher, Mrs. Brock, sent words of encouragement via e-mail and kept up on Dani's progress. Danielle's 4-H club, led by Sheila Beck who has a heart as big as they come, sent her a huge box filled with countless thoughtful items: a phone card, money, activity books, snacks, and more.

On Good Friday, Aunt Amy and Toni came to visit. Danielle smiled when she saw them and was excited to see the feast of chocolate muffins and strawberries that they brought for breakfast. All of us girls ate together and talked. You should have seen all the crumbs on her bed afterward, but it was so good, she didn't care. I hadn't seen her eat like that since we left home. I had prayed for joy for her. She had been so depressed for a couple of days. Thank you, Lord, for those ladies!!

Things were turning around. That day she only needed pain meds one time, and they took out her catheter. She even got out of bed and walked with help a short way. Physical therapy did arm and leg exercises with her in bed. She ate McNuggets for supper and a chocolate bunny for dessert. How healthy! Thanks to the Child Life Staff, Dani was able to do more crafts. She tried coloring, but she had to close one eye to keep from seeing double. We also began noticing some hearing trouble. We were praying both problems were temporary. Wanting to know the complete scope of things, we hoped that maybe we would get the full pathology report before Easter, but we had to wait until after the weekend. I wrote in my journal, "*I believe God for great things in His timing and that He'll receive glory and make doubters believe.*"

Kevin had to go home that afternoon and would not be coming back until Sunday evening. He needed to be home to touch base with our church and preach the Sunday morning Easter service.

More visitors came Saturday and more Easter presents. After all the visitors left, Danielle had an emotional breakdown and then started hyperventilating. She wanted to go home so bad!!

She was also missing her daddy. The nurses let her call him using the hall phone hooked up to an extension cord. Ahhhh, just the voice of her strong daddy calmed her down. We then set up a picture of him on her tray table. She drew a picture and wrote "Dad, Spencer, Sampson, and Scooter" on it—everyone she was missing.

Another CT scan, taken that afternoon, showed too much fluid on the brain. They began draining it at a faster rate. It looked like a permanent shunt would need to be placed on Monday. We were all hoping and praying that the ventricles would begin draining on their own.

Added to all the tubes, wires, and bandages was an ace bandage of sorts around Dani's neck. This was for the purpose of constricting the jugular veins to give more blood to the brain. Also, Dani's heart rate had been really low, which made her sleepy and sometimes confused. The added neck constriction helped to raise her heart rate, too. After a rough evening, I was hoping to wake up to a glorious Easter Sunday, full of hope and promise.

I awoke to a beautiful spring day and prayed as I walked briskly to the hospital, thanking God for the beauty of the skies and the flowers. I had spent the night at the Ronald McDonald house to get a good night's sleep in a real bed and had gotten up early to get to Dani's room before she could miss me. I tried the back hospital entrance I usually used, only to find that it was locked. I had to walk quite a ways to find an entrance I could open. It seemed like every entrance I tried was locked. I was in quite a panic to get to Danielle. When I finally did get in, my anxiety mounted as I made my way down several long hallways only to endure the wait of a few elevator rides. Time was ticking away. I knew she would be waking up soon, if she weren't already awake. I was elated to finally get to her room and hug her!!

It seemed to be one of the longest days of my life waiting for Kevin to get back to us. Danielle kept asking if it was almost time for her daddy to be there. We painted her nails, got her in real pajamas, and the nurses brushed out her snarled and matted hair to put it in pigtails. Anything to distract her! As the day dragged on, we colored, did crafts, and played games. We both desperately wanted to be with our church family worshiping God and celebrating His death and resurrection. The nurses found us a Kid's Praise CD to listen to. We sang along and prayed together and read the Bible. "I just want to be home celebrating Easter like a normal family," Danielle choked out as a tear slid down her cheek.

This hospital was filled with sick kids. Many, I'm sure, had the same desire. I was so unaware of how many people had gravely sick children until that week. Sure, everyone I knew personally was with their families, but I became aware of a whole new group of people who needed compassion and encouragement and God's peace in their lives.

When Kevin finally arrived, he had with him an enormous basket from my co-workers, who decided to bring Easter to us. They sent along such thoughtful things! Included were stamps, thank-you notes, and other items for the whole family. Of course there was Easter candy, as well. Kevin also brought library books to help fill my long days of waiting. Books have a way of transporting me into a world apart from my own. Escape from my hospital world was a welcome change. Danielle was excited about the basket of goodies, but she was more thrilled to be with her daddy. She told him that she never wanted him to leave again.

5

From Bad to Worse

*T*HE NEXT DAY WAS SHUNT surgery. When asked her name after surgery, Danielle touched her nose (something she was asked to do often during the recovery process). She was so out of it from the drugs!

After surgery, we found out that the results were in from the full pathology report of the removed section of tumor. Kevin and I nervously followed the doctors into a separate room. If they couldn't talk to us in front of Danielle, this had to be bad news. Our fear mounted as we sat down. The doctors shared the devastating, stomach wrenching news that her tumor was an Anaplastic Astrocytoma, grade 3. This type of tumor accounts for only 2-4% of all brain tumors and develops from star-shaped glial cells that support nerve cells. An Anaplastic Astrocytoma can infiltrate into adjacent areas of brain tissue as small fingers of cells, making it next to impossible to remove all of it. We were told that she would need aggressive treatment for this highly malignant tumor. Grade 3 tumors grow rapidly, so time was not on our side. After healing two to three more weeks, she would need six weeks of radiation and chemotherapy. That would be followed by a year of maintenance chemo. When the doctors left us alone, I held on to Kevin as if my life depended on it, and I cried until I had exhausted myself. We could see fear mirrored in each other's eyes. We had prayed so much in previous days, but we prayed with more intensity in that moment than we had ever prayed before. Desperate for a miracle, it was hard to wrap our minds around the fact that this was really happening to our family. We had served God faithfully and now this.

After composing himself, Kevin then made the dreaded phone calls to tell everyone the news and to ask for more prayer. I don't remember, but I'm pretty sure I probably slept by Danielle's side that night. I needed to be with her as much as I possibly could. We didn't tell Danielle or anyone else the statistics that were given to us that day for her type of tumor. Choosing to believe in our BIG GOD, and that with Him, anything was possible, peace began to erase the worry. When the time was right, we let Danielle know that she would need to go through some treatments and that her sickness was extremely serious.

The next day we met with a radiation doctor who answered many of our questions and showed us Godly compassion and even surprised us by praying with us. Options to think about were laid out before us. We were going to need wisdom that only comes from God.

Following the crushing news, Kevin's parents brought Levi down to be with us. We wanted to tell him in person what the pathologists found out about his sister's tumor. As we talked, the reality of the situation began to show on his face. This was the first time we had dared to consider that Danielle might not make it through this cancer alive. The three of us prayed, hugged, and wept together.

Just as we thought that we were done with surgeries for a while, a scan showed the internal shunt in a bad position. It had to be repositioned the next day. Dani screamed so loud and long the day after the shunt revision that the nurses had to give her Valium. Sometimes the head pain, especially the neck area, was so severe that she would scream uncontrollably. They said that was common with brain surgery patients, but as a mom, it was so hard to watch my daughter endure this. I would have to leave the room when the nurses came in, because I was sobbing and shaking so hard. My baby was in great pain, and there was nothing I could do. I couldn't kiss it away. When the pain was so intense, holding her hand was no comfort to her. All I could do was beg God for healing and mercy as I listened to those horrifying screams.

The song "Strong Enough" by Matthew West, one of Danielle's favorite singers, became my prayer.

"Hands of mercy won't you cover me.
Lord right now I'm asking you to be
strong enough— strong enough
for the both of us.

Cause I'm broken down to nothing, but I'm still
holding on to the one thing—
You are God and You are strong
when I am weak."

By now, Dani was doing physical and occupational therapy most days. Walking was difficult. It was almost like learning to walk again. She had to hold on to other people and have a belt around her waist that we could hold onto.

As if she didn't have enough to deal with, belly issues arose. Constipation began to be a major cause of pain. Danielle was introduced to the world of enemas and gritty fiber drinks.

We moved out of the ICU and into a regular room. Two weeks in the hospital already and no end in sight quite yet.

Danielle's hearing got her into some humorous situations. A doctor with a heavy accent and a voice we deemed as a "low-talker," asked her, "Now that you're twelve, how old would you have been five years ago?" "Two hundred and one," was her answer. Kevin, I, and the doctor were all baffled. Later we asked her about it. She thought the question was something about how old George Washington would have been five years ago. It was good to all laugh about something after days of Danielle screaming and crying. I was glad I slept in her room when in the middle of the night she blurted out, "I hate salad!" and when she cried out in a pouting voice, "You'd do it for Levi." Laughter truly is good medicine! She didn't remember saying either of those things, but giggled when I told her about it the next morning.

Soon Dani was smiling occasionally, and we saw glimpses of her old personality. She started staying awake more and eating and drinking enough to say good-bye to the IV fluids. She was on to using a walker and up to being wheeled around a bit in a wheelchair. After being in the hospital for 16 days, we were able to take her outside. Wow- the sun and fresh air never seemed quite so glorious! The trees were budding, and the birds were singing. Numerous smiles made their way to the face of Danielle that day. We had visitors that joined us on our outing—Kevin's parents, Aunt Kari, Kevin's sister, and Levi. We all ordered food and ate a picnic outdoors. It didn't take long before our little excursion wore Dani out, and we had to go back to our hospital world for her to nap.

There was an activity room close to us with games in it, so we would go down there and play when she was up to it. It became a good place for overflow guests to hang out. When Levi would visit, he took full advantage of the free hot chocolate machine.

In case I missed being a librarian, the hospital had a library. I started checking out picture books to show Danielle and some chapter books to read aloud. With her eye patch, she couldn't always read well, so I read to her.

By now, I was joining Kevin at the Ronald McDonald house every few nights so I could get a good night's sleep. One night I had to come back in the middle of the night, because Dani was crying and missing us. Most of the time it worked out, though, to leave at night when she was asleep and come back right away in the morning. We were also able to eat day-old Panera bread bagels at the in-house Ronald McDonald (RM) house for breakfast. Most days, supper was provided at the hospital RM house, or at the big Ronald McDonald house down the street. We hated to be gone from Dani too much, so we only used the RM house for sleeping, doing laundry, showering, and eating. We were so thankful to be recipients of that wonderful ministry.

After being with us for a week, Kevin had to leave again. Levi had stayed with us the whole weekend and had to get back to school, too. Lots of tears flowed as Danielle tried to hold on to Daddy and not let him go. Kevin shed a few tears that day as well. He was so torn between two worlds. He really needed to do some work and get Levi home, but he hated to leave his little girl who seemed so helpless in that hospital bed.

There was finally talk of going home soon. The financial situation was holding us up a bit. In our rush to get Danielle to Riley, we never thought about an out-of-state hospital being an insurance problem. Luckily, there were people working behind the scenes to get things straightened out so that our plan covered Danielle's stay at Riley. Now we had to start thinking about what treatment plan we wanted to do next. Doing radiation with a specialized machine in Indiana while working with the team of doctors we had grown to love at Riley was one possibility. The other was Danielle being part of a clinical trial in Cincinnati with a newer chemotherapy drug and using a more standard type of radiation. That decision was something we didn't want to think about too much just yet. Home was on our minds.

6

Home, Sweet Home

*D*ANIELLE COULDN'T HAVE BEEN MORE excited about going home to sleep in her own bed, spend time with her pets, and see her brother every day. Previously, these were things we all took for granted.

Dani was looking pretty rough after not having her hair washed for three weeks and not being able to brush it much because of her neck and head incisions. Nevertheless, smiles were abundant as we wheeled her out to the car. It felt so strange to be in a vehicle after not being off hospital property for over three weeks.

We got home on a Wednesday night right after church, so the youth group and some adults came to see us right away. One of Danielle's best friends, Kaitlynn, was among the group. She expressed how concerned she was for Danielle and presented her with a big stuffed bunny. Samson, our dog, was so thrilled to see us that he could hardly contain himself.

He moaned deeply and wanted our immediate attention. He then took several excited laps around the house before wanting us again. We had never seen him behave quite like that before. As soon as he calmed down, we got her rabbit, Spencer, out and put him on her lap. Contentment spread across her face and a few tears of joy trailed down her cheeks. Home, sweet, home!

My mother-in-law stayed overnight to help. She also left us a spotless house and a full fridge. Sleeping in our own beds was a luxury that filled me with gratefulness. Two-way radios kept us in communication with Danielle, as she needed us many times in the middle of the night. She still needed help getting up and walking.

The morning after we arrived home from Riley Hospital, Kevin was taking a shower and seeking God on Danielle's behalf. The shower was one of the few places Kevin felt he could express himself without alarming Danielle. While in the shower, he voiced his fears to God as well as his anger that such a beautiful girl who loved Him so much would have to go through such a trial. As the feelings of fear, anguish, and dismay mounted, Kevin continued to pray and ask for God's intervention. It was then that he was given a breakthrough. God's peace came over him in a way that he had not expected. Kevin heard the words in his heart and mind, "Danielle will be OK and your family will be OK." There was no question that God had spoken to him. He was certain that these words would prove true. He went from praying to worshiping, trying his best not to slip in the shower through it all. However, one nagging thought remained. What did God mean by OK? Why didn't he just say she would be healed, or that she was healed? Kevin accepted the fact that going to heaven would certainly fall in the realm of "OK." Yet he chose to hold onto the fact that "OK" could certainly mean healing. He often would wrestle with that question. Which would it be, heaven or healing?

We had never appreciated home more! I was on family medical leave from work to take care of my girl. First thing on the agenda was a trip to the beauty salon. We had a huge tangled mess on our hands! After dousing the back of Dani's head with olive oil and letting that soak for a while, off we went. The patient beautician spent a great deal of time trying to comb out the snarls. In the end, a big chunk of hair was cut out. Her hair had to be washed three times to get rid of the oily grossness and flakes from her scalp healing.

Double vision was a constant irritation. Our little pirate wore an eye patch over one eye at a time, rotating often. She also expressed, with out-of-character anger, how fed up she was of hearing us telling everyone about her cancer on the phone. We began to be conscious of going in another room to talk behind closed doors, and we asked for people to not call us much for a while. Danielle's peace was worth a lot.

Dani also wanted to eat constantly. Home cooking tasted heavenly after eating hospital food for a few weeks. We wanted to battle this cancer from every direction, so we ate mounds of fruits and vegetables, freshly made vegetable juice, vitamins, and whole grains. We limited dairy and meat and tried to eat sugar-free. The trouble was that we had a pile of sweets given to Danielle in the hospital and from visitors who stopped by. Not many days into our new eating plan, Dani was sobbing. I immediately rushed to her side and asked her if she was in pain. "No," she explained, "I just want to eat my candy." We decided to do one treat a day. I understood the torture of a chocolate candy bar in sight being a constant temptation.

Cards just kept coming. Word had spread of Danielle's situation. She got mail from Japan, the Philippines, and many of the states. A kindergarten class drew her pictures, Sunday school classes wrote her to tell of their concern and prayers for her. A young girl who went to my Aunt Marty's daycare even held a bake sale to raise money for Danielle. What a heart of compassion God had given that sweet girl! We continued to be amazed at how the family of God bands together in time of need.

7

Guidance From Above

*T*IME TO FINALIZE TREATMENT PLANS came quickly. We didn't even want to think about doctors and hospitals for a long while. We had been sent e-mails and been called about various treatments for cancer. One cure included boiling down a mixture of pure maple syrup and baking soda to ingest each day. It was disgusting, but hey—we tried it; anything that might help. We gave natural supplements, started vegetable juicing, and looked into treatment options. I was not in favor of chemotherapy seeping poison into her system to kill the cancer. The thought of radiation was equally scary. There were so many negative side effects from either option. We were going to need a lot of prayer. Countless people were praying for us, so we were covered there. This was a time for Godly wisdom. Our human reasoning was not going to cut it. God's plan, not our own, was what we wanted. We looked into gamma knife (highly focused beams of radiation), but that door closed quickly. Kevin and I both prayed until, after a few days, I approached him. "I really feel like we are supposed to do the clinical trial for chemotherapy in Cincinnati and the x-ray radiation there, as much as it scares me," I said. Here, he had heard the same answer but was waiting to see if my answer from God was the same, as confirmation to what he thought. Granted, this was not the decision my human reasoning wanted.

As soon as we talked to Dr. Fouladi, our new oncologist at Cincinnati Children's Hospital on May 1st, she had us come down a few days later for an updated MRI to see if a second surgery was needed. Dani's first surgeon wasn't able to get much tumor out and Cincinnati's neurosurgeon, Dr. Crone, was confident that he could get out a considerable amount more to improve her odds of surviving. (We were told later that this neurosurgeon took cases other surgeons wouldn't touch. Patients from all over the world came to him.) The surgeon would take measurements from the MRI to plan the surgery.

So Danielle would have something to look forward to before the next surgery, we took a trip to the Cincinnati Zoo. We originally thought a zoo trip would happen before we drove home from her first surgery, but she was not in good enough shape to do that at the time. By this time, she could walk short distances on her own. We took our time to enjoy some of Danielle's favorite things in life—animals. When Dani got tired, we sat to take a break. Working with animals was what she wanted to do when she graduated from school, most likely as a veterinarian.

After the zoo trip, we visited Kevin's cousin's house in Batavia, just outside of Cincinnati. This would be the first of many trips to the Winter's house. Some of their church members, who we knew well, came over for a "pizza and game" party. They even played Danielle's favorite game—Apples to Apples. All in all, it was a great day of "normal"—no cancer talk, lot of kids, loads of fun.

My prayer journal entry: May 5th, 2009

"Lord, I thank you for spring and the hope and energy of new life. You have been my strength, my hope, my rock when all around me is sinking sand."

Remember that conversation Kevin had with God in the shower? On one of our trips to Cincinnati, Kevin brought it up to his cousin Joe. He had told Joe how God had told him that Danielle would "be OK" and that his family would "be OK." Joe replied, "Now that you have brought it up, I also heard God tell me the same thing, specifically that 'Danielle would be OK'." He continued, "I did not want to be one of those people that make promises on God's behalf; I felt it was from God but did not want to confuse God with my own desires." Kevin knew what he meant, because he also would from time to time doubt himself as to whether God spoke to him or whether he was hearing what he wanted God to say. Kevin then brought up the matter of what does "be OK" mean? Joe revealed that he had struggled with the same question. God did not specifically say healed, but rather "OK." Perhaps if they were just hearing what they wanted God to say, they would have heard God say "healed" rather than to have to concede that "OK" could mean heaven. Either way, the question remained: does "OK" mean heaven or healing?

8

Here We Go Again

AFTER ENJOYING A FEW WEEKS at home, here we were, back for another brain surgery. This time we were at Cincinnati Children's Hospital and Medical Center. The night before Danielle's second tumor resection, Cincinnati hospital pathologists read the slides from Riley Hospital and thought the tumor was a grade 2 Fibrillary Astrocytoma. That was a much better diagnosis. We found that news out before the surgery. Whether that news would match with the outcome of the tumor samples sent out from this surgery or not, God was our firm foundation to stand on.

The private waiting room we had with family the day of surgery was peaceful and full of hope and laughter. We all knew God was in control. A hospital employee, who came to check on us often, said, "I can tell you are Christians. There is such peace present when I enter this room."

The neurosurgeon at Cincinnati Children's Hospital got quite a bit more tumor out during the brain surgery, but was not so aggressive as to risk any damage to the brain stem. Two samples sent off during surgery showed the same thing the pathologists thought the night before—a rare, slow-growing tumor. That would mean a shorter term of treatments instead of a year-long, as proposed. We all were excited and praising the Lord for a good report but we had to once again wait on a full pathology report of the tumor that was removed during surgery to find out for sure.

That night, knowing Danielle would sleep clear through, Kevin and I decided to take advantage of both sleeping together in the same bed and headed to the Ronald McDonald house across the street. Once again, we were thankful for a place where we were only a few minutes away from the hospital entrance.

Two days after surgery, Dani was starting to wake up more. She had such agonizing neck spasms that she screamed for a half hour. Even Valium wasn't enough to calm her. Finally, sleep came after a concoction of pain meds was given. There was talk of sending her tumor sample slides to John Hopkins for their opinion.

Another couple days passed with Danielle being awake more but still miserable. She wanted Kevin and me with her, but not to talk much to her or touch her. She was still not communicating, just moaning and not wanting to do crafts, be read to, or eat much. I felt completely helpless, lost and desperate for a way to bring Dani comfort and joy. Watching her like that was more than my mind could bear. My heart was breaking for her. Her suffering became my suffering, too. I prayed constantly!

After only a week, Danielle was released from the hospital. This time, she didn't have to learn to walk again and her body seemed to snap back considerably faster. Being home brought glimpses of joy and smiles. We were on the road to healing.

On May 28[th,] we took another plunge down our roller coaster of emotions. We learned that we were the "exception to the rule." The neurosurgeon had never seen a case where the pathologists say in the initial report that a tumor was a grade lower, only to have to come back after the full pathology report to say it was a grade higher. Danielle's tumor was a grade 3, according to the full pathology report, but parts of it were still a grade 2. Our year treatment plan as part of the clinical study would for sure be a reality. We started out before her first surgery thinking the tumor was a grade 1, only to be told afterward it was a grade 3. Before and during her second surgery we thought the tumor was a grade 2, and then after the full pathology report, we faced a grade 3 tumor. It certainly was confusing for our friends and family.

Just three weeks after being home, we made the trek back to Cincinnati to meet with the oncologist and later to get fitted for her radiation mask. Dani's doctor looked at her facial sores that were not healing properly. The tumor had caused one side of her face to be desensitized, so she didn't realize how hard she was digging when she scratched. Also, during the oncologist visit, Danielle experienced getting her first port access in her chest. What a nightmare! The nurse had trouble getting the needle in and had to use an extreme amount of pressure to get it in far enough. Dani was hysterical, shrieking in pain. I couldn't take anymore of watching my baby suffer, so my body said "enough" and just passed out. A couple more nurses were sent in—one for Danielle and one for me!

9

Our Home Away From Home

O<small>N</small> J<small>UNE</small> 2<small>ND</small>, <small>WE PACKED</small> our bags and headed to Cincinnati, moving in with Kevin's cousin's family for six to seven weeks of radiation and chemotherapy. Ginger and Mongoose, their small, cuddly dogs, were a huge comfort for Danielle. She and Ginger developed a special friendship. Ginger was a homely dog with a severe under bite and wiry, wacky hair, but Danielle gave her extra attention. Always sensitive to the outcasts in life—that was my Danielle.

Our first week in Cincinnati, Danielle was starting chemotherapy and radiation at the same time. She had to take oral chemotherapy capsules, as well as chemotherapy through her port. We were so thankful that our health plan covered the $14,000 of oral chemo that was given to her! Between the oral chemo and the pain pills Danielle was still taking for her headaches, she quickly became weary of swallowing pills. As for her radiation, it's a good thing Dani wasn't claustrophobic. Her radiation mask clamped on tight to the table, so she couldn't move her head at all. The week was without side effects from treatment, except tiredness and lack of appetite.

Praise the Lord; we were able to make it home every weekend, due to God helping Danielle's stomach to stay strong! Prayers were keeping me awake behind the wheel on those three and a half to four hour drives. The only physical thing that helped was an interesting audio book. Even then, the "sleepies" came over me often. Good thing Kevin didn't have the same problem when he came to visit. We were extremely thankful for the newer van provided to us. Dani could sit in one of the middle seats and lean all the way back. It made for roomier travel for all of us.

During the second Cinci week, Danielle started physical therapy and was given homework assignments. She was so exhausted; she didn't feel like doing anything. Even taking a walk down the street seemed to be a monumental task to her. Many foods she used to crave tasted disgusting to her. She rarely drank or ate without pleading on my part.

Danielle's attitude changed dramatically when Wrinkles, the Winter family's new American Bulldog puppy, was introduced into the family. He brought delight and entertainment to Danielle's otherwise dreary days. Wrinkles wanted to chew on everything—socks, shoes, water bottles. He would even tear the socks right off our feet! Sprinting around the room at lightning speed, Wrinkles was a ball of energy. He didn't realize that he was a huge puppy and would walk all over Danielle as if she wasn't occupying space on the couch. Tug-of-war was a favorite game for the two of them to play together when she wasn't letting him outside for constant potty breaks. Wrinkles became Danielle's exercise.

The third week we received some great news! After two and a half months of double vision, her vision had returned to 20/20. Other than the sores on her face, the doctors and nurses were surprised at how well her blood tests looked and how well she was doing. We, of course, gave all the glory to God and His protection!

Our fourth week was filled with early morning appointments. It was not uncommon to leave the Winter's house at 6:30 in the morning. Trying to get an exhausted pre-teen girl, with a body full of chemo and radiation, up that early was a real challenge! The dreaded port was used again after giving more healing time. Danielle was visibly nervous about the nurses accessing her port, but it went well, even despite some pain that was at least bearable. She got a slow feed of Avastin, which had the purpose of attacking the blood vessels that were feeding the very vascular tumor.

Sometimes we were at appointments from 7:00 in the morning until 5:00 in the evening. Time spent in waiting rooms was always such a joy—NOT! It made us appreciate our little clinic back home that always got us in within 15 minutes. We were not prepared for the hours of waiting we would do over the course of Dani's treatments. Sometimes we would wait so long for an appointment that it would be time for the next one to start, without even being done with the first one!

Despite the negatives of the fourth week, a dream came true for Dani. She got to pick out a puppy that would be her very own as soon as radiation was finished, and we could live at home again. A pocket beagle was her pick. Most puppies of that breed were ridiculously expensive, but we found a great deal on one that wasn't papered. We got to see his sweet picture online with paws too big for his body; big, flappy ears, and soft, brown puppy dog eyes.

Our fifth week brought news of why her nose wasn't healing. She had a staph infection. The forms of chemo that she was getting inhibited healing, so that wasn't helping the matter. Fatigue was worse now. No stomach upsets, but feeling "gaggy" often. It made her cough, like she'd throw up, but then wouldn't. We started noticing hair loss in the back of her head, but only the bottom layers closest to her scalp. With her having such thick hair, most people didn't notice. I tried to make her do her yoga homework, but being up off the couch gave her severe headaches.

Our skinny Danielle had lost six to seven pounds since her last surgery, which concerned the doctors. Dr. Fouladi told me to make her eat high calorie foods and to give her anything she wanted and was up to eating. Our healthy eating was already not quite as strict, but we finally decided to let her eat whatever she could, since sometimes radiation made so many things sound and taste awful to her.

Even at the beginning of the week, Dani was already missing our home, Dad, Levi and her dog, Samson. All the waiting rooms, appointments, and living away from home were getting old fast. We were so thankful to have a short week. Radiation was closed that Friday for the Fourth of July holiday.

Danielle was still helping to potty train Wrinkles, the puppy, so that kept her occupied between appointments. Thinking often how all the other kids she knew were having a fun summer, while she was spending hers doing cancer treatments, was a depressing thought. She was still not allowed to swim yet, so that was a bummer, especially since the Winter family had a pool.

Our family of four was together all that week in Cinci, so Dani got to have her daddy with her every day—such a big blessing that before we had always taken for granted. We had been going to Real Life Church on Wednesday nights. That week was their summer Vacation Bible School in the evenings, so we went to that while Levi helped out. On the last night, the teens presented us with a Wii Fit. Physical therapy at home would prove to be much easier with it.

We had a fun-filled weekend when we returned home. We went with one of Dani's friends, Maddie, to play putt-putt and stopped at a specialty ice cream shop afterward. Dani and her dad played on the Wii a lot too. This was all fun, but it wore her out!

The next week was our last full week of radiation. Unfortunately, the week got off to a rough start. Danielle threw up a little during radiation. She didn't tell the nurses or me. When we were getting in our van to leave, a nurse came running out to make sure Dani was alright and explained that she was cleaning out the mask and saw vomit. She told Dani how sorry she was and to please wave to them next time anything happens. (We're so glad it never happened again.) Since she couldn't move her head at all during radiation, I was sick to my stomach just thinking of her having to endure throwing up and maybe almost choking on it.

A couple days later, we decided to do a girls' day out, just the two of us, while we still had the sights of Cincinnati nearby. On a rare day of only one appointment, we headed to Newport Aquarium to marvel at God's underwater creatures.

We even got to pet some small sharks as they swam around in a shallow pool.

Shopping for her new pocket beagle puppy was another fun part of our week. Danielle's excitement was building. She decided to keep his given name, Gizmo. I think dreaming about getting her puppy so soon, and looking at the pictures of him posted online, carried her through the last few weeks of being away from home.

10

A New Normal

Monday, July 20ᵗʰ, 2009, was a momentous day for Danielle. It marked her last day of radiation and brought the thrill of packing up to move back home for good. On our way back to Bryan, Ohio, we stopped to pick up her new best friend, 9 week old Gizmo. He was so tiny and a little bony. The rest of the way home, she had a huge, contented grin on her face as she doted on her little lap companion. It was wonderful to be home again, especially knowing we wouldn't be returning to Cincinnati for a few weeks. When Kevin and I prayed with Dani before bed that night, Gizzy snuggled up to her and she declared, "This is the best day ever!"

The weeks following were filled with puppy training and chasing after Gizmo. Who needed exercise when you had a puppy to take care of? What did Danielle ever do without him! This was her chance to be a mommy, and Gizmo was her baby. The first time she had to go back to Cincinnati she cried about leaving him with her brother all day. In her eyes, nobody could love and take care of her baby like she could.

That summer, Kevin's parents sold their home and moved to Bryan to be close to us in our time of need. It was convenient to have family just minutes away! Mom Boulis is the kind of person who loves to help people. I think she was born to do that—it is her mission in life. She is happiest, when at the end of the day, she knows she has lifted someone else's burden. We also realize what a sacrifice that was for both of them—leaving friends, church family, and neighbors behind.

In August, Dani started her year of maintenance chemotherapy. Her nose was still trying to heal up, and ear problems had been plaguing her. The trouble with the ear was that she couldn't feel pain on her left side, so she could have a horrendous ear infection and not know it until fever set in. I learned to routinely check her ears to at least make sure the outside wasn't swollen, red, or seeping. We also found out that Danielle's profound hearing loss in her left ear was permanent, aside of a miracle.

As part of the clinical study, Danielle and I periodically had to fill out questionnaires, and Dani had to take a computer test. After a while, it was annoying, but I figured that if it helped someone else later on, it'd be worth it.

School was about to start again. She had missed the entire last quarter of 6th grade and the whole school knew about her cancer. She just wanted to be a 7th grade wallflower, afraid that everyone would ask her about her surgeries and tumor.

Being back in a school routine was good for all of us. The teachers knew that Danielle would be gone every other

Thursday and possibly the day before, as well. Most gave her assignments early and she worked on them while in her hospital bed getting chemo or on the van trip. Some nights she got home well past her bedtime and she still made it to school the next day. It was perfect that she had choir 1st period, so she could sleep in a little and miss that on Friday of treatment weeks. Dani pushed herself to keep up with homework and never made excuses. She would go to school tired, rather than miss classes. When kids came to class with lame excuses of homework not being done, the teachers thought of Danielle and how she had a valid excuse but didn't use that to her advantage. This was another example of her wanting a normal life as much as possible. She wanted teachers and fellow students to treat her as if her cancer did not even exist.

Blessing us by opening up her home, an old friend of mine, Laurie, just happened to now live almost halfway to the Cincinnati Children's Hospital. When we had early morning appointments, we would stay over at her house the night before, or if we got on the road late and were overtired, we'd stop before going home. Usually though, Danielle was on a mission to get to Dad and her pets ASAP; so even if I was sleepy, we rarely stopped after appointments, only before the early ones. Danielle began to look forward to her stays at Laurie's where she was greeted with homemade treats and could watch Disney channel and Nickelodeon on a big screen TV in bed. Her early morning awakening was made better by having a big breakfast complete with donuts. What a treat! After the first time of seeing Dani's face light up in response to eating donuts, it became a tradition. Dani's only regret to being at Laurie's was leaving so early in the morning.

In September, my cousins Vicki and Darla, along with many helpers, put on a benefit concert with a silent auction and ice cream sundae bar at their church. We soaked up the encouraging songs by Kate Jordan and Soul Venture. The highlight for us was the whole church praying audibly for our family. I bawled like a baby. We felt love filling us to overflowing at that moment. The whole night we were overwhelmed with blessings. It was humbling to be the guests of honor. I much prefer being the giver and blessing others! By the end of the night, Danielle had a painful headache. Kevin and I told her that with all the prayer, maybe God was doing something in her head and healing her.

By this time, Danielle had only thrown up once from chemo, so she decided one day to try her oral chemo without the anti-nausea medication. Big mistake! Since her life was so out of control, I let her be in control and decide this on her own. When she threw up all evening, I deeply regretted that decision. She never tried that again and had a new appreciation for her nasty tasting, melt-under-your-tongue medicine.

Around the same time, Janis, previously a complete stranger to us, was almost finished decorating a "dream" bedroom for Danielle. Janis had heard about Dani's cancer and decided to use her talent for decorating to bless our daughter. Danielle got to choose the color scheme and the comforter. Her lime green, aqua, and chocolate brown room was gorgeous and the coolest twelve-year old's room ever! Janis thought of every detail—handmade pillows for on the bed, a bulletin board, picture frames that tied the colors together, a valance that matched the pillows, lamps, and matching white furniture. Daydreaming about her room gave Danielle something to keep her mind occupied and to look forward to. We spent hours together pouring over pictures of bedrooms in decorating magazines and books, and searching for comforters online. As soon as we closed on our new house, Janis transformed Danielle's empty room into a masterpiece. Danielle got to help put the furniture together, but she couldn't see her room until it was all finished. It was like revealing a room on the Extreme Home Makeover TV Show!

We had applied for a Habitat House shortly before Danielle was diagnosed with cancer. The place we were living in needed a lot of major work and was not worth fixing up. The house belonged to the church Kevin pastored, and we needed more space for our kid's classes, so it was being turned into a building for that purpose. Long story short, Habitat for Humanity was building us a house. That meant after long weeks in Cinci, we would spend our Saturdays working on the new house. It was more than I could handle sometimes, and I had more than one emotional breakdown over this. I still look back and wonder how we put in the hours on the house that we did while caring for Danielle and spending so much time in Cincinnati.

Since Dani had started chemo, one of our daily prayers was asking God to protect her good tissues and organs and that the chemo would only get to the brain tumor. Four months into treatments, the nurses were amazed at her blood work. Usually by that marker, patients start having trouble with numbers on their blood work. Stacey, the best nurse coordinator around, ran a two page report every time, and Danielle's numbers were usually all in the normal range or at least close. She really was not getting sick to her stomach now that we had learned our lesson with the anti-nausea meds.

In October, Grandma Miriam accompanied Dani and me on a three-day Cincinnati trip. We played games like Yahtzee, Skip-Bo, Racko, and other card games, and we devoured lots of snacks when we weren't at appointments. That helped our trip seem special and made it bearable for Danielle to be away from home for a longer period of time than usual. My mom and Danielle always had a special connection stemming from the three years that we lived with my parents when Danielle was between fifteen months and four years old.

During this Cincinnati visit, she had an upper GI procedure done to see if there was any physical reason why she couldn't seem to gain weight. That chalky-tasting drink was not at all pleasant, but we were glad that it all seemed to go down like it was supposed to. The doctor started Danielle drinking some high-calorie juice drinks that were not exactly yummy, but Danielle thought they were better than the thick, milky alternatives. By the time of her next appointment, she had gained 1 ½ pounds, so no appetite stimulant was needed.

The ENT (ears, nose and throat doctor), at this point, thought that her nose wouldn't heal much more until after she stopped having chemotherapy treatments. Her nose had started to bleed every day from the sores around it. This was highly annoying, but she had to endure it for several more months.

Despite everything, Dani got all A's and one B on her first grade card for 7th grade. We were so proud of our girl! The Bryan Middle School staff was awesome! They worked with us on all appointments and were completely supportive of our family.

During Dani's "down in the dumps" days, Gizmo became a huge comfort to her. She started developing more headaches around Thanksgiving, but soon after, she started wearing glasses and that seemed to help.

Christmas was a joyful lift for Dani. She was trying to find just the right present for everyone, as usual. She picked out a comedy DVD for her dad and an Elmo T-shirt for Levi. Flavored coffee and nuts were chosen to give to her grandparents. Pets were included in the gift-giving experience, because, to Danielle they were a huge part of our family and she wanted them to have a special day, too. She bought both of the dogs enormous bones to gnaw on while we were away at Christmas celebrations. Turning up the Christmas music, Danielle and I set up the nativity scenes, hung the stockings, and spruced up the house with holiday decorations. Over the course of December, we whipped up some chocolate-mint fudge, capital crunch candy, homemade hot cocoa mix, a cheese ball, and Chex party mix. Trying to make things as normal as possible, we immersed ourselves in the joy and wonder of celebrating our Savior, Jesus, coming to earth to be born a baby. One of the most special gifts of Christmas for Danielle was getting to sleep in during the two-week break from school. Ahhhhh.

11

A New Year

2010 BROUGHT A NEW HOPE for a better year. We were filled with gratitude to God for walking so closely with us through our valley, and to all of the many people praying for our family. We believe it made a huge difference! Danielle was looking good and had a better attitude than she had several months ago. We chose to walk by faith and not by sight, that God was doing a work in her brain stem. We were confident of the power of our God and His plan, however that would unfold. Our financial needs were being met in amazing ways. When we needed a listening ear or some encouragement, it was always there. Our life had found a new normal, and we chose not to dwell on cancer as the focus our lives revolved around. For Danielle, being in school and at church with her peers were good ways of making life seem as normal as possible.

Just a few days into the New Year, we were driving to a family get-together when Danielle exclaimed, "Why did everything get louder all the sudden?" We assured her that it didn't and turned off the radio. After testing her, we found that she was definitely hearing a little out of her left ear that was previously deaf. We were praising God all day and told everyone we knew of her miracle.

On the other hand, Dani's nose took a turn for the worse. Enough so, that the hospital decided to delay her chemo schedule a week to let her nose heal. Oral antibiotics were given, and we had more cream to slather on.

MRI results the end of January showed that Dani's tumor measured a bit smaller. Praise the Lord! We couldn't have been happier, except for if the news had been that the tumor was gone completely.

Our Danielle turned thirteen in February. That meant she could finally have a Facebook account. She had been anxiously awaiting that for a year or more. Also, we got word that her Make-a-Wish laptop computer would be ready in a few weeks. Danielle's oncologist had submitted her name to this amazing organization several months before. After exploring all the possibilities—meeting a famous person, taking a trip to Florida to visit her friend Rachel, going on a shopping spree, getting her own laptop, or fulfilling a lifelong dream, she chose the laptop since it would help her in everyday life instead of just being fun for a few days. (She almost went with the trip to Florida, since she wanted to see Rachel so much.)

Danielle loved having Grandma Miriam join her in the back seat for her birthday week trip to chemo. Her IV didn't go so well for blood-work and ended up being sore for a while.

Add to that, her gusher nosebleed on the way home from Cincinnati, and it seemed like we had enough excitement (good and bad) for one week.

We did get to stop at Laurie's on the way home. She showered Danielle with fashionable presents—an Aeropostle shirt and jeans, orange flip-flops, and a cool, brightly colored striped purse. When we got home, Grandpa Ralph took her out to Myro's Pizza Buffet for a birthday treat. So in Danielle's mind, the good far outweighed the bad that week.

Stubbly hair was starting to appear under her other layers of hair in the back. She had missed her thick hair, so it was nice to have that hope of having thickness soon.

By March, Dani was up to 88 lbs. Despite an ear infection, she was doing quite well. Kevin and I were taking turns, as much as possible, making the drive to Cinci. The two to three day trips I usually did. I actually looked forward to those, because it meant extra time with my girl, since I was off work. I hated driving, but if that's what it took to be with her, I did it.

At the end of March, Danielle got her Make-a-Wish. Tim, our Make-a-Wish "go to man," and another representative from their fabulous organization, took our family and our good friends, the Hartman's, out to eat at Danielle's favorite Chinese buffet restaurant. After our bellies were full, we watched Danielle open up mounds of presents. That organization really knows how to do things up right! She got a desk, a chair, a carrying case, a printer, paper, cool software, a MacBook Pro computer, a web-cam and an Intuis drawing pad. Wow!! We just had to wait a few more weeks for the last present—a year of Internet access. This gift enabled her to

Skype with her best friend, Rachel, who had moved to Florida in 2008. They could also Facebook and e-mail more, too.

The whole family got to go to Danielle's appointment in Cincinnati together during spring break. Compliments of a church member, we had received tickets to the Creation Museum, so we stopped there before heading back home. God's imagination is mind-blowing when we consider all His creation!

One of our spring visits, we found ourselves having two days of appointments with a free day in between them. We were excited to find out that the hospital had free tickets to the Cincinnati Zoo. What could be more perfect than Danielle getting to spend a day with animals? In lieu of waiting rooms, we were blessed to see a seal playing with a ball, an entertaining lorikeet, countless other animals, and a gorgeous tulip display.

Our "cherry on top" for the day was shopping. We found an identical pair of shoes to her favorite orange plaid canvas ones that had fallen apart. We had previously looked all over for a similar pair to replace them, but with no success.

MRI results the next day showed the tumor had shrunk 1/10 of a centimeter. We were hoping and praying for more, but it was still great news!

Unfortunately, not more than five minutes on the road home after chemotherapy, Danielle began throwing up. I was not prepared at all, since this never had happened before. She filled the cup we had in the van by the time I pulled into a gas station to get another cup. I must have picked the only station without fountain drinks. We just had to dump the vomit outside and reuse the cup until I found a place with cups.

I then remembered my mother-in-law's friend, Treaundra, lived in Cincinnati and was a nurse. We called and were able to stay at her house for several hours until Dani could travel again. After a while, Dani ended up needing another prescription to stop the vomiting. Poor girl! She was so miserable. Treaundra took such good care of both of us. After that, we were even more thankful that this was not the normal chemo side effect for her, as some patients experience.

Daddy was also a hero that day. Dani was missing him and asking for him so much that he came with his dad and met me half-way home. I got to relax in the passenger seat with my father-in-law while Kevin drove his little girl home. Once again, she found such strength and comfort in her dad.

> *Prayer entry from Danielle's devotional diary:*
>
> *"Dear God, I pray that you will help me endure the "fire" of my chemo and brain tumor, and I trust you to make something good come out of it."*

12

If It's Not One Thing, It's Another

*Y*OU'D THINK THAT DEALING WITH a child with cancer would be enough and that the rest of the family would be free from all sickness and pain, but that's not the way it was. Our long hospital walks became increasingly difficult for my knees to handle. I ended up getting a helpful cortisone shot in one of them. Along with my knee pain, I had developed neck problems, and found out I was in full menopause at age 37 (had started having symptoms when Dani got sick). Kevin had developed an eye twitch that came and went, depending on the stress level at the time. We knew that these things were minor compared to what Danielle was dealing with.

Danielle's blood work still looked "perfect." Seventh grade was over, meaning more time with Gizmo and to play on her new computer. The summer that stretched ahead of us was a welcome break from the rigors of school days.

What we thought would be just a day trip to Cincinnati in June ended up as a hospital stay for an ear infection. Dani had said her ear was hurting her the day before we left. I figured the doctors could just look at it when we got there. She woke up at Laurie's the next morning with a fever and ear pain so awful that she couldn't open her mouth enough to eat donuts. I called ahead to the hospital. They immediately canceled her MRI and instead ran antibiotics through her port as soon as we arrived. The infection was looking pretty bad, so they also delayed chemo. By that time, Dani's ear was swollen shut, so they put a wick in her ear to drain it. Despite the pain meds, Danielle screamed like I hadn't heard her do since recovering from her craniotomy. It broke my heart to be so helpless to alleviate her pain.

After the ear calmed down, the MRI was done. Great news! The tumor had shrunk even more. It was now 2/10 centimeter shorter and 1/10 centimeter narrower.

After two days in the hospital, she got to walk down to the gift shop with her IV pole. There waiting for her was a huge stuffed Gizmo. We splurged and bought it right then and there. Back in her room she snuggled that thing in her hospital bed and talked to it like he was really Gizzy. That became her pal that had to accompany us on every Cinci trip. After three nights in the hospital, Danielle was more than ready to go home.

The end of Dani's year of maintenance chemo was in sight. With four more chemo appointments to go, she was thinking about cake to celebrate the end. But first, we had a weekend trip to Kevin's cousin Charlie's house in Eastern Ohio. We all attended the Alive Music Festival there. Levi was excited about many of the Christian bands that were performing, and Danielle was most looking forward to seeing her favorite comedian, Tim Hawkins—live. Almost as much fun as that was our all-girl trip with Charlie's wife and daughter to Hot Pots to paint pottery. Danielle chose a cute little dog bank to paint.

The only problem Dani had before the end of chemo was her nose. The vascular system was dying as a result of Avastin, one of her chemo meds. The ENT doctor was concerned about the septum (middle of her nose) perforating, resulting in a hole there. We prayed for God to reverse that process and waited to see if it would hold out for the last two treatments. On the flip side, we had news that after her maintenance chemo was finished, she would be totally done with all chemo. We would only need to come every three months, as long as Danielle was doing well.

13

Time to Celebrate

*J*ULY 29ᵀᴴ, 2010, MARKED THE end of chemo. We had celebrated the previous night at church with the youth group. Cake and ice cream for all! Dani had to taste the foul medicine as the last chemo flowed through her body from her port. Sucking on LifeSavers helped a little. (This is common for some chemotherapy patients to have a nasty taste in their mouth during the infusion, even though it is not taken orally.) After the chemo was over, several nurses came in the room, along with some Child Life Staff. One was blowing bubbles and all of them had on funny hats and were clapping and singing:

> *"I don't know, but I've been told,*
> *This chemo thing is getting old.*
> *The best thing is that now you're free,*
> *The worst thing is we sing off-key."*

They presented her with gifts of nail polish, an art kit, and a notebook. Wow—a day worth celebrating!

We had to go back two weeks later for an MRI, some other appointments, and to meet with her oncologist to discuss the next few months. Thanks to the blessings of my friend Mary, we went out to eat at a nice restaurant on the way home.

Back in Bryan the next day, Danielle got a big surprise when she answered the door. A deliveryman handed her a bouquet of balloons and candy. The card said, "Happy last chemo! From your friends at the library." I felt extremely blessed to have such thoughtful co-workers.

Caring Bridge Journal: July 31, 2010

> *"Wow, what a journey we've been on so far. We are so looking forward to not traveling to Cinci so much. God has been with us every step of the way and has protected Danielle beautifully from most side effects of her treatments. Our life is getting more normal all the time. Danielle is back to music lessons now. She is taking guitar again and her school year should be much better with actually being there most of the time."*

Not usually a vain girl, Danielle was starting to be concerned about the appearance of her nose and scars on her forehead. We went to the salon where the beautician, Sarah, gave Danielle more bangs to cover up some scars. Sarah also tried to help out with the spiky hair growing in that had a mind of its own. She did Danielle's make-up too, to show her how to conceal her nose scar. Perfect! The confident smile on her face spoke volumes! Then it was off to the dentist to get fitted for Invisilign to straighten out those teeth.

A couple weeks after her last chemo, we headed to Cincinnati again for an MRI, follow-up, and ENT appointment. Her nose was healing up already after only being off chemo two weeks. The tumor measured as stable, not enough change to note. Danielle was so thankful to go a whole two weeks without needle pokes, waiting rooms, or four-hour van trips—something most kids wouldn't even think about.

Perfect attendance for the first quarter of school felt wonderful to Danielle. Even though it proved to be a tough quarter, she was awarded for her diligent work with all A's. She loved having no make-up work, not having to miss 1st period due to late night drives from Cincinnati, or not having treatments that made her feel "wiped out" much of the time.

By the time we had to return to the hospital the end of October, Dani was up to 94 lbs. and had grown to 5'4". All the staff commented that it was the best they had ever seen her look.

14

Hope and Pray

WE WERE NOT PREPARED AT all for the news we received the next day. The tumor had grown. We didn't know what that meant yet, but possibly more chemo if an MRI in two months showed more growth. The growth was minimal, but it was still considered a progression according to the neurologists. We decided not to tell Danielle about the negative news.

From a journal I wrote to Danielle, to tell her story: October 27, 2010

"Dad and I are amazed at how well you are doing. God has been so gracious to you. He loves you, Danielle - His precious daughter. We hope you've learned to trust Him more through this difficult time. We praise Him through the good and the bad, but it's in the hard times that

*our faith is strengthened and Godly character
is built."*

Caring Bridge Journal: October 29, 2010

*"We are still trusting in God for the outcome,
knowing He is in control, and He knows what
He is doing. Would appreciate all of you praying.
It would be an awesome Christmas present to
go in December and find it had shrunk again,
or better yet is gone completely. We know God
is capable of anything."*

We had a wonderful autumn day watching both our kids take part in a Quinceanera for a friend from church. Danielle had a haircut scheduled that same day, so I asked if Sarah could do a little something special, since Dani would be all dressed up. When I picked her up, she took my breath away with how grown up she looked in a full updo. Sarah really outdid herself. I was so grateful that my girl got a chance to spend a day looking like a princess. Wow - she was gorgeous! As time drew near to the start of the ceremony, Danielle adorned herself with her floor length evening gown. Who would've thought that she would be able to find a fancy black dress at a second-hand shop that would fit her size 00 body? God even cares about the little details! She wore heels for the first time and carried herself beautifully. Both she and Levi had to take part in their first dance after the ceremony. Neither was excited about dancing, but they did it for their friend Jade's special day.

There was smooth sailing in the Boulis house until the beginning of December. Danielle started complaining of her left eye bothering her. She described the feeling as how a body part feels after it has been asleep and is trying to wake up. No vision changes, just felt annoying. The oncologist was not concerned, but said it could be tumor related. The eye started feeling better after a few days, but it still felt weird to her.

Kevin had the thought that it might be like when a nerve is pressed on for a long time and "falls asleep." When the pressure is no longer there, it "wakes up." Maybe this was a good sign after all.

Danielle trusted God completely. She could feel His love and strength—that much I am sure of.

> Danielle's Personal Journal: December 11, 2010
>
> "I just got back from watching the new Narnia movie. It is the third in the series. This one was my favorite. C.S. Lewis has a brilliant mind. He uses symbolism beautifully. A lion, Aslan, was the perfect symbol for God. He is loving. I get a warm feeling when he talks."

My Dani had a Snoopy Christmas. Almost every gift she opened had Snoopy on it. Ever since her Grandma Ann bought her a Snoopy t-shirt a year or two ago, she had decided to be a Snoopy fan. She doodled Snoopy characters and wore Snoopy shirts as much as possible. It became our mission, when shopping in Cincinnati after appointments, to find Snoopy paraphernalia, especially t-shirts.

A few days after Christmas, we headed to Cincinnati as a family. Due to a full house already at the Winter's, we stayed in a hotel and tried a new restaurant, Johnny Rockets. It was good to be all together for a few days away, even if it included a hospital appointment.

The devastating news of more tumor growth made our stomachs turn.

CaringBridge Journal: December 30, 2010

"I must say I was very discouraged today. Praying so hard since Oct. for the tumor to shrink and for amazing results today. I am always so hopeful, since I know God is capable of anything. Don't know why we are going down the hard road instead of her being healed now. God sees the big picture and we don't, so we still trust Him, as always. God gave me some encouragement tonight, though. After we got home, I opened a jewelry box I had shopped for in Cinci with a gift certificate. When I opened the drawers there were 2 bracelets inside. This was obviously not supposed to come with free jewelry and was all sealed up. One of the bracelets had the words of **Isaiah 41:10** *on it.* **"So do not fear for I am with you. Do not be afraid for I am your God. I will strengthen you and help you. I will uphold you with my righteous right hand."** *I believe God knew I needed to be reminded of those words today. It's still hard now knowing what the next few months will bring, but it helps knowing God's promises are true and He will be with us every step of the way.*

Thank you Lord!!"

The first week of January 2010, Danielle started on a new clinical study with a chemotherapy called MKO 752. The protocol was all oral chemo, seven pills at a time. She had to stay at the hospital for twenty-four hours for observation after taking her first dose. Child Life Staff kept us occupied with a Yahtzee game, stained glass crafts, more games, etc. Dr. Fouladi, by law, had to make sure Danielle knew not to get pregnant while taking this. If you knew Danielle well, that was extremely laughable. Thankfully, there was no nausea or other side effects from the chemo, so we got to go home. We began praying, once again, that the chemo would only affect the brain tumor and not her good cells and organs.

Williams County Cancer Assistance began helping us out with gas cards for our trips to the hospital. What a blessing!

Aunt Amy got to accompany her niece on one of our trips. They helped me stay awake while driving by asking me questions from the "Are You Smarter Than a Fifth Grader" game. Danielle loved having her special aunt with her. We even got to stop for one of Dani's favorites on the way home—Bob Evan's stacked and stuffed blueberry cream pancakes. What can I say, the girl loved her pancakes! For Danielle's fourth week of chemo, she had to swallow 22 pills! The pharmacy was out of 200 ml pills, so she had to take the only two we had left plus 20 of the 50 ml pills. We did it in shifts, taking little breaks in between. UGH!! As a person who loathes taking pills, I felt so bad for her. She actually did it with minimal complaining. What a trooper she had been through all the medical stuff she had to endure.

15

Gotta Have Faith

S PIRITUALLY, DANIELLE WAS ROCK SOLID. She would sing praise songs to Jesus in the shower, even if she was not feeling well. She also would strum her guitar while singing worship songs she learned at church, from the radio, or from Mike, her guitar teacher. I asked her, while living in Cincinnati, if she was mad at God or asking, "Why me?!" Her reply was, "I just figured, why not me?" People get cancer all the time, good people included. She never seemed to question God about it or blame him for it. She just accepted it as an unwelcome intruder in her life, and that she needed God to be her strength to get her through.

Danielle's Facebook: January 27, 2011

"I don't want to gain the whole world and lose my soul." (a quote from a song by Christian musician, Toby Mac)

A week later, we noticed Dani looking unbalanced when she walked, and she began drooling. She stayed home a day from school with a severe headache and some dizziness. Cinci hospital got her in for an MRI right away. Kevin and I both went with her for that. Dani really did not want to go and insisted that she was fine. MRI results showed more tumor growth. The new chemo wasn't working, so she stopped taking that.

At that point, she had not lost her sense of humor, hence, her random musings on Facebook. Levi has a great sense of humor, too, and always kept things on the funny side for Dani's sake. She was developing quite a sense of humor herself and surprised us with her quick wit, at times.

> *Danielle's Facebook: February 2, 2011*
>
> *"How do aliens get the supplies to make a flying saucer?"*

Laughter is good medicine, and many times it took our minds off our situation.

After lots of prayer, Kevin and I decided not to try any more chemo. The chances of the tumor responding to a different kind were less than 10%. Even so, we relied heavily on God's wisdom and not our human reasoning. Valentine's Day was Dani's last day of school. She tried going back the next day, but she didn't last long due to headaches. Looking down seemed to make them extremely painful. Her speech was also starting to be a little slurred. Within a couple days, Danielle was having some trouble swallowing and was choking a little.

The next week marked her 14th birthday. Her English teacher had students and teachers make Danielle birthday cards to cheer her up. The art teacher had different kinds of Snoopy pictures printed off so that most of the cards had a Snoopy picture on them somewhere. My sister, Amy, and our good friend, Toni, joined us mid-week for a day. They brought chocolate muffins, strawberries, and lunch with them. In the hospital, Danielle had that exact breakfast with them and thoroughly enjoyed it, so that was a special treat for her to have again. We all played games and had a good dose of laughter for our weary souls.

The next day my co-workers sent Danielle birthday balloons with some gifts. That brought a smile to her otherwise dreary day. She tied the balloons around Gizmo and watched him struggle to get them off as he ran through the house. Now that was entertainment!

We tested her walking by going to the pet store. Due to a lack of close parking spaces, we had quite the test! She had to stop often and hold on to whatever was handy to steady herself. We walked arm in arm all the way back to the car until someone passed. She was trying to look "normal" and would let go when people were driving by.

Great Aunt Jane and Uncle Larry had sent her ice cream money as a birthday treat, so we got to go to Eric's All American Ice Cream, her favorite place. That girl would eat ice cream every day if she were allowed!

We were thrilled to find out that a traveling evangelist, who has been used in the gift of healing often, was in town. Kevin called him, and he agreed to come to our house to pray for Danielle the day before her birthday. The whole family gathered together that Saturday, even my brother's family from Wisconsin. We prayed fervently for God to heal Danielle. Each person there had great hope and faith in our God's healing power to take over in Danielle's situation. Healing would be the most awesome birthday gift Danielle could ever receive!

Meeting Baby Jeannie, her only girl cousin on the Aufdenkamp side, was a huge thrill for Danielle. Ever since she heard they were coming, she couldn't stand the wait. When Jeannie was placed in Danielle's arms, it was a special, memorable moment. She had always wanted another girl cousin to balance out all the boys.

We celebrated a day before Danielle's actual birthday with a butterfly cake that Aunt Amyjill, my sister-in-law, bought. The administrator of the library brought over cookies that his wife had made for us—perfect for our houseful of people. We were crammed in pretty tight in our tiny home, but the love that flowed that day was priceless.

> My post on Danielle's Facebook wall: February 20, 2011
>
> "You are the daughter God knew I needed in my life. I love you more every day! Praying that your next year will be the best one yet!"

Sunday after church, Levi was driving a friend home from church when he hit an icy spot on the road. He ended up hitting a small tree and totaling our car. We were so thankful that neither he nor his passenger was hurt. I think that sent me over the edge emotionally! I already had enough stress in my life without that.

Danielle missed going to school and wrote of that often on her Facebook page. She was so bummed that she wasn't getting well enough to go back to school for that extended amount of time. We tried to keep up with homework, as best we could. She truly even missed her teachers. I must say, she had some wonderful ones.

Kevin and I took the next week off work to be with Danielle at all times. She had to drink with a straw and had more incidences with choking and swallowing. We had to resort to thicker drinks, like chocolate milk. Lots of sore throat days became common. Her double vision had returned, and walking was getting worse. Things were going downhill fast.

Danielle with her rabbit Spencer (Easter 2008)

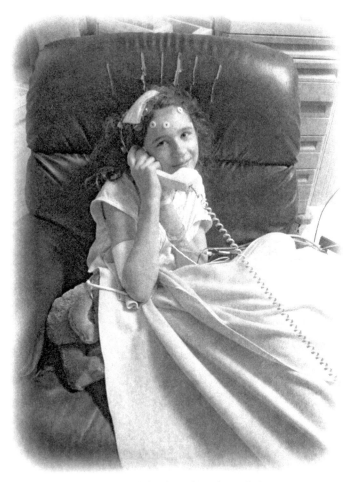

*Talking with her best friend, Rachel, at
Riley Hospital (April 2009)*

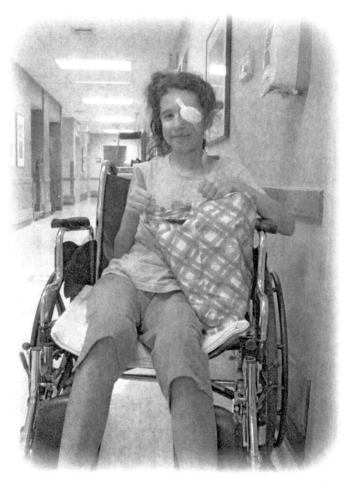

Happy to be leaving the hospital after 21 days (April 2009)

Celebrating her 13th birthday with her cousin, Grant (February 2010)

Danielle and Melanie at the Cincinnati Zoo (May 2010)

Hiking at Oak Openings with Grandpa Scott (September 2010)

Levi and Danielle at a friend's Quinceanera (October 2010)

Reading Snoopy Birthday cards from her classmates (February 2011)

Dani and her daddy on her 14ᵗʰ birthday (Feb. 2011)

Danielle meeting her baby cousin, Jeanne,
for the first time (Feb. 2011)

16

Desperate For A Miracle

O N THE SPUR OF THE moment, we decided to pack up some things and head to New Jersey to attend the Bay of the Holy Spirit Revival Meetings that were taking place there that weekend. Borrowing a wheelchair, we drove off. We were basking in God's strong presence at the services. We worshipped for hours and praised the Lord until late into the night. We were able to bring Danielle up front to be prayed for. She experienced what is called in Pentecostal circles as being "slain in the Spirit." While worshipping God and being prayed for by Evangelist Nathan Morris, Danielle had experienced an overwhelming sense of God's power that caused her legs to buckle. As she started falling, the evangelist caught her and eased her onto the ground where she lay with eyes closed, hands in the air, and a noticeable grin on her face. When asked what she experienced, she indicated that she was simply overwhelmed with amazing peace.

On another occasion at the revival, one of the elders of the church, along with his wife, prayed with us. While praying, he had been given a vision from God. The vision he shared with us was of Danielle wearing a beautiful white dress and dancing. A little confused at what that meant, we continued praying. On one hand, the idea of Danielle being able to dance was exciting. It certainly could be revealing her healing. However, Kevin and I both were less than enthused about the "white dress." It hinted toward imagery of heaven. Either way, Danielle would "be OK," and we, while certainly having our preference, still realized that this too could mean heaven or healing.

The second night of the revival, we saw a lady that we had talked to the night before. She had been in a wheelchair 30 years and was slumped over. Tears flooded my eyes when she was able to get up out of her chair and walk, haltingly. Later on, we saw her sitting up straight in the pew. Many healings took place those two days, but we brought Danielle home with no change in her physical state. Our spirits, however, were renewed. God had done some work in our hearts. We trusted that Danielle's healing would come in God's perfect timing.

CaringBridge Journal: March 5, 2011

"Very discouraging week. Not sure what God is up to. We were so sure He was healing her and we would soon see results. Danielle is so weak and not up to doing much. Her walking is worse and her left arm and hand don't work well. Had a rough night Thursday night and all day Friday. She was extremely dizzy and

felt miserable. Lots of tears. We are so thankful
she could sleep well last night and had a better
day today. My dad bought us a little seat to
sit in the shower. We got her cleaned up today.
She couldn't do everything herself, so I had to
help her. Lots of tears during that process. On
the bright side, she is swallowing better. The
steroids she started taking must be helping. She
is having trouble swallowing pills, but food and
drinks seem to be going a little better.

Danielle likes to have Kevin or I with her on
the couch much of the time. Grandma Miriam
came and stayed with her Friday, so she had
Grandma right beside her all day and my
mom was able to fix meals and do dishes so
I could spend time snuggling with Dani. She
is going through a scary time right now and
needs us more than ever. She had some teary
moments before bed. I stayed with her tonight
when I tucked her in because she said she didn't
want to be alone. She had me read stories to
her tonight too. It is breaking my heart to see
her go through this. Really need to see God
moving and working on her behalf. I feel like
God is silent now, but even though we don't
see Him working, we praise Him anyway. God
is our strength, comforter, joy, and peace - our
everything! Praying for better days ahead! Also
looking into the Burzynski Clinic in Texas.
They have seen some success with brain tumors.
He has some non-conventional treatments and

has some clinical trials going on with those. Not
sure what to do right now for her. Not sure she
wants to leave home to do any type of further
treatment. Need some wisdom from the Lord
on what to do. Wish I knew His timetable and
His plan!"

I started working part-time so I could be with sweet
Danielle more. Home health nurses had started coming,
along with speech, occupational and physical therapists.
When the occupational therapist asked Dani what she missed
doing, she broke into tears. Her left arm became so useless;
she had to lift it with her right arm to move it. Her speech was
getting progressively more difficult to understand. Singing
wasn't possible anymore. She missed that as well as playing
her guitar.

Family started coming to visit and help out on a weekly
basis, especially Grandma Miriam. She would come and
play games with Danielle when Dani was feeling up to it.
Grandma Miriam also helped Danielle cut out and decorate
cookies. Grandpa Ralph came often, too, to see his precious
granddaughter. A few friends from school came to visit,
as well as the teens from church one night after service.
Cards were pouring in from everyone—friends, family and
strangers. Some had gifts of money. All were assuring us of
their support and prayers. It reminded me of when she was
first in the hospital. We had quite a collection of cards from
then, too. The flower shop down the street began making
deliveries regularly to our house. A young boy from school
even sent something for her. The mayor stopped by to give
her a card and a City of Bryan pin. Many others stopped in to

pray with Danielle. It began to be discouraging for her to have people pray and nothing seemed to get better.

By this time, we were using the wheelchair for Danielle anytime we left the house. Due to her lack of mobility and not being able to use her left arm at all, she was limited in what she could do to occupy her days. Kevin and I decided to get cable TV for her, so she could watch, "I, Carly," "Good luck, Charlie," "Phinneas and Ferb," and other Nick or Disney favorites. We also watched every episode of the "Cosby Show" from the library. That became one of the few things anyone could do with her. We'd sit next to her, snuggle up close, and watch a few shows.

All signs were pointing at going to the Burzynski Clinic in Houston. Since theirs was an alternative treatment, the insurance would not be covering anything related. We sent Danielle's medical records to Texas and set up a consultation as soon as they were received and looked over. One of the school guidance counselors, who had been so supportive of us all along, spearheaded plans for a spaghetti dinner fundraiser. This was the third fundraiser for our family; the second one being a bluegrass and gospel concert with a chili dinner at our church. The spaghetti dinner brought in almost exactly the amount we needed to pay the Burzynski clinic to start treatments. A God thing? I think so! Danielle felt awkward at the spaghetti dinner. Her friends and classmates were so excited to see her and talk with her. One-sided conversations are hard to keep up, though, since Danielle could only nod. Most of the food she couldn't eat, and we had failed to bring a thick drink along with us. Needless to say, Kevin and Danielle didn't stay long. I stayed to visit with some of the 600 people who had shown up to support our family. Once again, the town of Bryan made us proud to be a part of this great community.

Courtney, the same guidance counselor who put together the dinner, also made a video of Danielle's teachers, friends, and other Bryan Middle School staff. They all said, "Hello," and, "We miss you," and wanted her to know of their love. When Courtney dropped it off, there was a framed picture of the 8th grade students holding up papers that spelled out, "WE MISS YOU DANIELLE." She desperately needed those messages from her school, and they meant a lot to our whole family.

17

Texas, Here We Come

*T*HE FOLLOWING WEEK WE WOULD leave to travel the long road from Northwest Ohio to Texas. Lots of preparation needed to be done before we left. Dani used a wheelchair with a shopping basket at the store to pick out bones for each dog to give them on the day we left. She also said, through tears, that she wanted to do something special for Levi. I think she felt bad that she got all the attention and that Levi was left out. That was Danielle, always feeling for others. She picked out some of his favorite snacks to make up a basket and used some birthday money to pay for it. We had developed a comfortable way of communicating, despite her lack of understandable words. Learning the sign language alphabet and some other basic signs years ago proved to be helpful for our whole family.

Every day that week was a day with a new surprise, it seemed. Two days before the fundraiser, Danielle received a package in the mail. Actually, it was for our whole family, but definitely contained lots of cool items for Dani. She excitedly opened two new Snoopy shirts, Snoopy pajamas, socks, flavored chap-sticks and a few other goodies. Grandpa Ralph had told some of his business affiliates about his precious Danielle and her battle with cancer. They wanted to do something special, and they really went above and beyond. In the box were various gift cards for gas, restaurants, and Wal-Mart. We were amazed at the generosity of strangers who had never met us but poured blessings our way. We thank the Lord for each and every way someone blessed us, whether great or small. It was all appreciated.

The day before the dinner, huge baskets were delivered to us, as well as a bag of groceries. It was all intended to help with our trip. One basket was specifically for Levi, as he would be spending time home alone without us, so he could go to school and live life as normally as possible. It was filled with many of his favorite snacks and some gift certificates. We were thrilled that someone would think specifically of Levi. That meant so much to him, too. As with other siblings of kids with life-threatening conditions, all the mail and gifts come to the sick child. Rarely is much thought given to the emotionally vulnerable child left home with at least one parent missing to take care of the sick child. In Levi's case, he was old enough to understand and be fine with it all, but I'm sure it was hard for him to watch his sister suffer. The basket for the rest of us was filled with things for our van ride to Texas. Someone put a lot of thought into that basket—very unique ideas. Lots of soup was included with the food. That was something Danielle could still eat. We just had to thicken the broth if it was too thin for her.

Nance, a thoughtful coworker of mine, gave Danielle some balloon flowers she made, and she also went together with another coworker to give her a pet treat basket. That came in handy for the trip, since Gizzy was traveling with us. Another co-worker, Deb, took Dani's rabbit to care for him while we were away. All of the wonderful people I work with were supportive and encouraging along the way. I thank the Lord for each one of them!

On March 29th, we arrived at our hotel in Houston. Just when we thought we couldn't stand another minute in the van, we were free to walk around in the warm Texas air, but too tired to enjoy it yet. Our first day at the Burzynski clinic lasted from ten in the morning until five at night. To brighten our day, there was a bouquet of cookie flowers awaiting us at the hotel. My Aunt Marty had phoned a local Assembly of God church and told them we'd need a church home while in Texas. They were thoughtful enough to welcome us to Houston in a tasty way.

Luckily, the first week we were gone, Levi was on a missions trip with a neighboring church. God had worked that out perfectly. At least he wasn't home alone all spring break.

Our first few days in Texas were depressing. We were awaiting lab results to see if Danielle would for sure qualify for antineoplaston treatment, a non-toxic way of treating cancer. Nothing was going right. Danielle was losing bladder control (that had started on our van trip). We had to re-schedule the MRI. It seemed that Houston was not used to having her type of brain shunt, so many offices did not have the equipment to reprogram her shunt after an MRI, which was absolutely necessary. We also found out that Danielle would be getting a feeding tube and needed a different port that would have access outside. Both of these surgeries would require extra money that we didn't have yet. God provided for both of these and more through a church friend, a business connection of my father-in-law, Scott, and the donations of countless individuals.

After four nights at a cramped hotel, we were more than ready when an old high-school friend of Kevin's invited us to stay at his house for the remainder of our stay in Texas. Kevin enjoyed reconnecting with his buddy, Todd. His house was a bachelor pad, for sure, but we were thrilled to have a fenced-in backyard for Gizzy. I had a real kitchen to cook in, once again. The only disadvantage to the house was having to carry Danielle upstairs every night for showering and bed, and then down again in the morning. Even at less than 100 pounds, she was dead weight.

I had been sleeping with Danielle every night, so that I could know when she needed me. She would elbow me or tap me with her good arm. At that point in time, I would've considered an uninterrupted night's sleep a dream come true. Danielle's weak bladder had us getting up often. She also could not position herself well to get comfortable, so I needed to adjust her body often.

With her not being able to move much, I began massaging her whole body, especially concentrating on her legs and feet. She asked for foot rubs often. I learned some techniques from a video to help me better understand what to do. I studied a book on reflexology to use on Dani's feet. We also did arm and leg exercises to continue with her therapies.

Faith Assembly Church took us in. The church family all began to pray for us. The first Sunday there, we were given a miniature rose bush and greeted warmly by many sisters and brothers in the Lord. Many offered to help in any way possible. Kevin went to a Bible study and some extra services that Danielle was not up to attending. We were so thirsty for God's presence in our lives and needed Him desperately. Honestly, we were wondering if we had made a mistake in going to Texas. Had we heard from God wrong? Did we want a cure so much that we just thought that was what we were supposed to do?

As if in response to our doubt, God began opening up doors of ministry. Kevin was able to share the hope of having Jesus in our lives with a few people in the waiting room at the Burzynski Clinic. I got to share with a nurse at First Street Hospital about Jesus being the only way to get to heaven in response to her comment: "It doesn't matter what god you believe in, as long as you believe in something."

After a week in Texas, Danielle was more tired and couldn't suck from a straw anymore. We had to start spoon feeding thick smoothies to her, but spooning beverages just resulted in choking. Dani didn't even have the strength to cough properly. It didn't take long for Danielle to be homesick. She missed Levi terribly, along with her pets she left back home.

We were thankful that the clinic let Gizmo come with us to most of her appointments there. It's always good to have a best friend by your side.

The day of the MRI that we had rescheduled, called around about, and waited for, finally came. We weren't on pins and needles about the results of the MRI; it was just protocol to have it done before Danielle could start her anti-neoplaston treatments. We arrived home from that appointment and

were greeted by a big stuffed bear and ball
Dayspring Church secretarial staff in Bowling
That brightened our day a little, though it was ge
to read Danielle's face for emotions. She couldn't si
anymore. Her face muscles were slowly losing contr

We were also starting to get mail at our Katy,
address. Healing scriptures were opened that day, as
as gifts of money to help cover our mounting med
expenses.

Kevin and I were starting to fight a lot over Danielle's
care. The stress was building and we were taking it out on each
other. The tension was awful. Caring for Danielle became a
24-hour a day job. Many tasks took both of us, such as getting
her to the bathroom. If one of us left to run an errand, we
might be called to assist after just a couple of items were put
in the grocery cart. More than once, we just had to leave the
cart there and rush home.

We were so thankful when the feeding tube was put in.
Now she could get more in her besides applesauce, pudding,
runny oatmeal, yogurt, thick smoothies, and baby food. I had
read up on foods that fight cancer, so I knew what nutrition
to put in her tube. Asparagus was at the top of my list, along
with other fruits and veggies pureed. The hospital thought
the clinic was going to teach us how to use the feeding tube,
but the clinic nurse at our appointment the following day did
not know how to care for a feeding tube. We ended up having
to teach ourselves with you-tube videos and explanations off
the internet.

Once home from the surgery for the feeding tube and
chest catheter, we set up a bedroom for "the girls" in the living
room. We borrowed an air mattress from Todd's friends for

Boulis

I was getting up in the middle of the night to
me in the night, as well, so I would have clean, dry bedding to put on the next time around, despite having two sets of everything. Todd's washer would need the reset button pressed several times for each load, since it would randomly stop. All this was exhausting me to the point of insanity. I would get so frustrated when Danielle would tap me or honk at me just when I finally got back to sleep. I would wake up and cry, being so tired I couldn't even think rationally anymore. The dose of steroids she was on to keep brain swelling down, kept increasing. At every increase, it became harder for her body to sleep. The less sleep she got, the more she needed me for various reasons all night long.

As if we needed more stress, the hot water heater went out just a few days after Todd left on a ten-day vacation. His buddy that would normally fix it was on vacation with him, so we just had to suck it up and figure out how to deal with it. Todd hooked us up with a couple he knew, in case we needed to call them for showering at their house. After three days of not showering, we were desperate and called those complete strangers. Sponge baths were all we could do for Danielle at that point, due to her lack of mobility and the medical paraphernalia she was hooked to. We washed her hair in a blow-up basin that let us do that task while she was on the couch. When our hair got too gross with the Texas heat, we'd heat up water on the stove to also wash our own hair in the blow-up basin. Washing dishes also required heating up water on the stove. I just pretended it was "Little House on the Prairie" days.

Danielle's stomach took a while to heal from the feeding tube. She also had a Hickman catheter put in her chest the same day, as well as the removal of her old port. The big stuffed bear came in handy after surgery. We placed that bear so that it covered both of her incision sites, so Gizmo wouldn't step on those spots and hurt her.

The day after surgery, we had Danielle in the ER for severe stomach pain. Turns out, she was severely constipated. I ended up having to resort to suppositories when nothing else worked. Sweet relief! Honestly, we felt like having a party to celebrate.

CaringBridge Journal: April 5, 2011

> *"God woke me up and had me read the part of Exodus, in the Bible, where Moses kept asking Pharaoh to let the Israelites go free. There kept being more and more plagues and finally there was a breakthrough and there was freedom. This plague of illness keeps getting worse and worse, but there will be a breakthrough sometime. Also read about how the blood of a lamb covering the entrance of the house protected the Israelites*

> *from death coming to their house to take the*
> *firstborn. Jesus' blood is covering Danielle's life*
> *since she has accepted Jesus Christ as the Lord*
> *of her life and has been forgiven of her sins.*
> *Because of the blood of Jesus shed for us on the*
> *cross, she will be protected from death, maybe*
> *not physical death, but for sure spiritual death.*
> *She will not have to pay the consequences for sin*
> *(being in hell), but Jesus paid that consequence*
> *for her with his death on the cross. Good to be*
> *reminded of. This suffering will not last forever,*
> *and she is covered with Jesus."*

Dani discovered a new way to give herself a voice. She could peck out a sentence with her right hand and make a voice on her computer read it out loud. The first time she did this, we were sitting in silence when a deep, manly voice said, "I am craving a sub sandwich." We also saw her type to a friend, "I wish I could be normal."

On April 11th, Dani started antineoplaston treatment. She started with a small dose that would increase over time. Treatments were every four hours round the clock. Being disconnected to the portable medicine pump only happened once a day, while the medicine bags were changed. All three of us would go to the clinic for Kevin and me to learn how to flush her central line, take blood samples, program the medicine pump, keep everything sterile, and the tedious job of preparing medicine bags. We did that every day for a couple weeks. It felt like medical school. Our nurse was impressed with how fast Kevin caught on. In no time, he was the quickest rookie "bag prepper" there. We were on a mission—to get Danielle home by Easter. That was her written wish.

Each day, I pureed up fruit, veggies, and kefir to put in her feeding tube. I made sure I got as many cancer fighting foods in her as I could. We used lots of "green things" like spirulina, wheat grass, barley grass, and chlorella. I did my research, reading several cancer fighting books. Dani could still eat a little by mouth. No matter how much we gave her, she still wanted more. Most times, it would all run out the side of her mouth, even though we closed it for her. She still wanted the taste of food, though. Drinking was not an option at all anymore. It took some major effort to rinse out her mouth after eating, but like everything else, we found a way.

Before we left for Texas, a butterfly habitat I ordered came in the mail. Danielle had indicated she wanted one for quite a while. I thought it might prove to be a welcome distraction, and it did just that. Every day in Texas, I brought the mesh habitat to Danielle for her to watch. The caterpillars made quick work of the food and grew enormous compared to how tiny they were when they started. Soon the chrysalids were formed. We kept busy enough, that before we knew it, it was time for the butterflies to emerge. We fed them bits of watermelon, oranges, and sugar water. Flitting around in their home, they gave Danielle a glimpse of beauty in her life, which seemed otherwise bleak and void of all beauty. When the butterflies needed the freedom of the big, blue sky, we released them. Danielle watched them flutter away.

CaringBridge Journal: April 19, 2011

"Let our butterflies that we had been raising go free today. Was neat to watch them complete their cycle of starting off as caterpillars and becoming beautiful. That cycle always reminds

me of how our lives are without Jesus Christ. We go about our day thinking that is all there is, and when we are willing to die to self and surrender to what God wants us to be, He turns our lives into something beautiful.

I realize life doesn't always seem beautiful all the time. Just because I'm a Christian doesn't mean my life is easy or wonderful all the time. I struggle often. I don't always fly high like I'm intended to, and I don't always reflect the beauty of Christ like I should, but I know that my life with Jesus Christ is WAY better than it would be without Him.

I have struggled lately with my relationship with my Lord, Jesus. Asking a lot of "whys" and not " feeling" like He is close to me many times lately. I know love is not a feeling, but a choice of how I act, so I praise Him anyway, even if I don't " feel" like it. Even if I don't feel like He is answering my prayers. Even if I haven't seen any glimpses of healing lately for Dani. I know this "dry season" will not last forever and there will be a breakthrough someday. I also know His ways and thoughts are higher than mine and I choose to trust Him with my life and my family. That said, life in definitely a struggle right now, but God is able to bring us through this."

At our consult with the nutritionist at Burzynski, my bubble was burst. Here I thought I was doing everything right for Danielle, but she wasn't getting enough calories. Dani was put on a formula called Jevity. I still supplemented with all my "power" foods, though.

Our down time was filled with worship music, reading the Bible, and reading mail to Danielle. We were given a couple Hardy Boys Mysteries, so we read those aloud on our trips to the clinic. Drawing, watching TV, and pecking one-handed on her computer, were the only things she could still do to pass the time. I would take marker caps off for her and replace them. The fat ones were easier for her to hold, as she was losing some function in her right hand, too. All the drawings came out looking like a first grader had made them, which was a little frustrating for Dani, but it didn't stop her from doing it. On a hard day for me, she painstakingly colored in block letters on a paper that said, "I (heart) MOM." The tears fell as I saw what she had written. Here was my little girl going through the most awful experience I could imagine, and she thought to encourage me and let me know that she loved me. That was typical, sweet Danielle.

She also made a paper that read, "I miss Levi." She hadn't seen him in three weeks. Any other time we were gone, he could come to visit, so it didn't seem so hard. Levi was always her comic relief, and since they were both teens, they understood each other. We had Skyped with Levi once a week, but he was busy with track season and school, so weekends were the only time we talked to him at length. I missed him terribly, too. It was hard to have my heart in two places, knowing that I was missing his track meets and being a part of his daily life. I wanted to be there to cook his supper and hear about his day. We were relieved to find out that a few friends had some hangout time with him a couple times a week, and he ate supper with Grandpa and Grandma Boulis occasionally. I had to look at it as Levi's preparation for adult life, so I wouldn't feel so bad. I told myself it would be good for him to have to fix most of his meals, do his own laundry and dishes, shop for groceries, etc.

Danielle was oftentimes plagued with constipation, which was very painful for her. We would try everything else first, but most times ended up doing a suppository. When every other bathroom emergency ended up in wet clothes, we begged for a catheter to be put in. The day before we left for home, my prayer was answered. We finally got some sleep that night! I could've kissed those nurses that took such great pains to put the catheter in. It was not an easy process, which did not surprise us by this point. Nothing went according to plan while we were in Texas.

18

House Turned Hospital

WE WERE BACK IN OHIO the night before Easter. The three-day trip home was one of painful headaches for Danielle and constant finger spelling of "out." Her upper body and head didn't have much control anymore, so I had to sit in the back and hold her in her seat. The seat belt didn't help. Any turn, no matter how slow, and any stop, would make her start falling out of her seat if we didn't hold onto her. By the time we arrived home, we never wanted to set foot in that van again. My back and neck hurt from sitting sideways to steady Danielle, and we all felt like walking zombies.

That first night back, we started our new routine of Danielle sleeping with me in my bed, while Kevin took her bed. I had to switch sides so her right hand was beside me, in case she needed to poke me. After being poked every five minutes until two in the morning, I got her in her wheelchair by myself (not an easy feat), leaned the seat back, and we took a stroll around the block in our pajamas. I figured if we couldn't sleep, we might as well do something. Getting her back into bed, I read cards to her from the stack of mail waiting to be opened. I am embarrassed to say that I lost it that night, emotionally. I was determined to keep her awake at that point, since I knew that as soon as I tried to fall asleep, the elbowing would start again. When she would start to dose off, I would remind her, in words laced with anger and stubborn frustration, that she wanted to stay up all night. I apologized many times for that night and wished I could have taken my angry, stubborn attitude back. How could I have been so selfish?! She couldn't help the fact that the steroids made her stay awake, or that she needed to change positions often, or that she needed to sit on the bedside commode, trying to relieve her constipation in the wee hours of the night. I knew then, that if I was going to be a good mom to Dani, I would need some help during the day, so I could get some sleep. I pleaded with God to help me through this and to comfort Danielle as well.

Only Kevin and Levi attended Easter service at church. A little later, we all were able to make it to Kevin's parents for a family get-together. Dani had to sit in the La-Z-Boy while everyone else ate Easter dinner. My heart broke as I saw tears in her eyes while we were eating. I knew how much she wished she could be eating and drinking and sitting around the table. I questioned our choice in coming to the meal. I felt like I should just sip Ensure in solidarity during her formula feeding, instead of enjoying a feast.

Easter evening, Danielle threw up at bedtime. She vomited several other times in the night. Keeping her from aspirating, we placed her on her side all night. Morning came with a trip to the ER in Bryan. She had accidentally (we think) pulled the Hickman Catheter out of her chest. Whenever we transported her, we were so careful of the tubing connected to her central line, afraid that it would rip out of her chest and be a bloody, painful ordeal. We were in a panic when it happened, but it turned out to not be a big deal at all.

Communication was lacking that day between hospital staff as we loaded her up to travel to a hospital in Toledo. We waited not so patiently for five hours, only to find out that we would have to go back to Bryan to have a PICC line put in her arm until the hospital in Toledo could schedule a time to place a new Hickman Catheter in Danielle's chest. This whole twelve-hour trial had meant missing three antineoplaston treatments. At least when we arrived home, my parents were waiting there with supper ready. Also waiting for Danielle was a balloon attached to a cute little bear that had been delivered earlier that day.

Sodium and potassium levels were a constant watch. If either sodium was too high or potassium was too low, we had to stop treatments until levels were back to normal. Blood tests were done three times a week to check those levels, along with other vital information.

Home healthcare nurses stopped in every other day to check on Dani and helped us with various issues, such as her Foley Catheter. The catheter would make her terribly itchy and cause discomfort. Many times, it had to be changed before the scheduled time, due to infection. Between formula fluids and the antineoplaston fluids, her fluid output kept us hopping to keep up with emptying the bag. The nurses suggested a bed wedge to help keep her head elevated enough to ward off headaches in the night.

Help was pouring in by now. Kevin's mom helped out a lot toward the beginning of the week. My co-workers began a rotation of bringing us supper every Wednesday night. My mom and sister would come over on Thursdays. Mom would stay through until Dad came to get her on Saturdays. That was a good excuse for Grandpa Ralph to get to come see Danielle every week.

One of Grandpa Scott's business associates, who had already been a huge blessing financially to us, wanted to do something special for Danielle. I told Wendy about an American girl bed Danielle had been wanting. A few days later, the bed arrived, along with a couple outfits for her Samantha doll. Soon after, more outfits arrived; hand-made this time. Every day, I would ask Dani what outfit Samantha should wear and dress her in it. Samantha would sit and watch TV with Danielle or rest in her new bed. I tried to let Dani help dress her doll, but usually it ended up that I did most of it myself.

Dani's steroid dose was upped to control her twitches. Forming finger-spelling signs was becoming increasingly more difficult. We had to resort to eye movement communication and used a series of homemade charts to help us figure out what she might want. When her eyes moved rapidly up and down, we knew we had our "yes" answer. I can't imagine how frustrating it was for her to get her thoughts across to us with our deluxe "20 questions" game.

Danielle was mesmerized by fish swimming in a large aquarium in the waiting room at our monthly visit to the pediatrician. Then and there, we decided to dig out our fish tank from the attic as soon as possible. On Mother's Day, after a pancake breakfast (courtesy of Levi) and church services,

Kevin and I took Danielle for a wheelchair ride to the pet store. We bought a male beta that she named Squiggles. It took quite a while to figure out which fish she wanted and what name he should have using our "yes" and "no" eye communication method.

A few days later, my Aunt Judy sent money to get Dani more fish and a little water frog. My sister Amy and I picked out two colorful female betas and a miniscule brown frog. We set the tank up right next to her and positioned her to gaze at the little swimmers often. Watching her fish, listening to music, and watching TV were the only things she could do. We read Scripture to her daily and sometimes a chapter of an interesting book.

We had traded a life of baking cookies together and taking the dogs for a walk to positioning her in a Hoyer Lift to get from the bed to the couch, feeding her through a tube, and wiping her bottom. If only I could have turned back the clock to have at least one more normal day with her.

By mid-May, I was completely overwhelmed with our life. On a daily basis, I needed to: give her meds, give her massages, change positions often to prevent bed sores, perform mouth stimulation techniques, and exercise her neck, arms, legs, and feet. Added to that, I had to keep her Foley area clean, feed her, give lots of water through her tube, empty her Foley bag, transport her from bed to couch and back to keep her comfortable, do the slow process of figuring out what she needed, and keep pillows just right to keep her from being a bobble-head and her body from flopping over. Also, I was making sure her arm brace was worn a few times a day, keeping her nails short so she didn't hurt herself when her hands clenched up, making sure her feet stayed elevated most of the time, cleaning her mouth out with oral swabs several times a day, and trying to get her outside for some sun every day.

As if all that wasn't enough to handle, Danielle had a boil that turned out to be MRSA and needed to be cleaned every day. My heart would literally ache for my girl, knowing there was nothing I could do to alleviate her suffering. I begged God for mercy on her plight. Each night, as I crawled in bed next to her, I realized how special she was to me. I prayed for my daughter, knowing that my love for her couldn't be expressed in its fullness with mere human words.

By June, Danielle lost the ability to regulate her body temperature. An alternating pressure mattress topper was delivered, which helped her feel more comfortable, so much so that she began spending most of her time in the bedroom. We were still battling MRSA sores, but they were healing. Breathing treatments were started to help her coughing to be more productive. Stomach problems were beginning. Her formula was not digesting well.

My parents stayed with Danielle every other Sunday, so I could attend church services and lead the worship music. The opposite Sundays, Mom Boulis came so I could lead worship and then come home. I was nervous about staying any longer, in case Dani had to sit on the commode or needed a diaper change or any other task that required a second person.

CaringBridge Journal: May 30, 2011

"Was so good to lead worship at church yesterday. This is therapeutic to me to play piano and sing. Worshiping God makes everything seem OK when I am lost in His presence. I am

bathed in joy and peace when I am worshiping
- nothing better!!!!!! Am always sorry to see it
end and go back to the real world."

I began reading parts of the book of Job every day to Danielle. I figured she could relate. I knew I could. I just kept thinking, "The worse she gets, the greater the miracle will be," or, "Maybe this is a time of testing to see if we will stay faithful to our God."

CaringBridge Journal: June 5, 2011

"I have not been strong this week. May have appeared it to others, but have been very irritable and upset at myself Friday for being late on some things for Danielle. Felt like coming up with organized thoughts was like wading through pudding toward the end of the week. Ashamed to say I haven't been the easiest person to live with. Finding fault with others when I have made just as many mistakes. I really need God to fill me with love and compassion right now for others...and patience. Thank the Lord that when I am weak, He is strong!"

19

The Beginning of the End

*M*ONDAY, JUNE 6TH, DANI WAS admitted to the hospital for IV fluids after having the blood tests show a sodium level of 173. Of course this meant going off treatment once again. I was grateful to let the nurses give Danielle her meds and feedings. I even got to read a book.

Being at the Bryan Hospital had its advantages. Grandma Ann came every day in the morning, so I could go home and clean up a little. Grandpa Scott, too, was able to come several days on his lunch break. This enabled me to go for a walk outside and him to have special time with his granddaughter. Levi could pop in, even if it was just a short visit. Kevin spent the evenings with us and came every morning, too.

Blood and urine tests at the hospital both showed MRSA. That meant gowns and gloves for everyone except Kevin, me, and Ann. We had been around her, cleaning up vomit, diarrhea, spit, etc. before we knew she had it, so we already had been exposed. We still washed our hands constantly, especially upon leaving the room.

On Dani's seventh day in the hospital, she had a special visitor. The charge nurse let Kevin bring Gizmo up on a leash. Dani was very emotional when we told her the day before that he would be coming. She couldn't make a facial expression to show her emotions, but the little moan and a few tears let us know how she was feeling.

It was the last day of school for Danielle's classmates. We had been invited to a last day assembly, if she was up for it, but with being in the hospital, that was out of the question. Later that day, someone stopped by to present her with an award for having a GPA that was in the top 10% of her class. (Danielle had been in the top 10% of her class as of February, when she had to quit attending school. Winning this award was an 8th grade goal of hers, so they gave her an honorary award, even though she wasn't able to complete the school year.) She also received a DVD of the 8th grade slide show and Chicago trip. Our Dani was voted, "most courageous." One of her classmates had written a poem about Danielle that was read at the assembly. We were honored to read a copy of it.

She Is
She is the girl that every young, teenage
woman would want to be.
She has the personality that everyone
would dream of having.
Even though she is weak, she is fighting the
toughest battle that she has ever fought.
She may have been quiet and shy at
times, but the love in her heart
sang like the loudest bird on a beautiful spring day.

**She is beautiful, caring, and loved every person that
she encountered as if they were her best friends.
She is inspiring and stronger than anyone could ever be.
Every day she faces a new battle, but her
strength and the people around her
help her to keep moving forward through
every one of those battles.
Her smile and happiness warm people like a fire.
No one can describe this young fighter in
any other way except by her name,
Danielle Boulis.**
Written by Hannah Wieland

After more than a week of being in the hospital, Dani was able to return home to her best buddy, Gizmo. Sampson, our Springer Spaniel and German Pointer mix was ecstatic to have her home, too. A hospital bed was moved to the middle of our living room. She was still hooked up to IV fluids and taking IV antibiotics. We were encouraged to keep up with using a massager to keep her congestion loosened up. After a couple of days of being home, Dani was back on her antineoplastons. Despite being home, she seemed sad.

God knew we needed something to brighten our day and add laughter to our lives. Gizmo loved being in bed with his "mommy." One day, after getting in her bed, he stretched out his paws, only to have one of them land on the bed control. All of the sudden, Dani's feet started lifting up. I could tell she thought that was hilarious. She couldn't really laugh, but I think she was trying to. Gizmo raised and lowered her head a few times after that day, but the first time was definitely the funniest.

Having her sleep in the living room in a hospital bed meant that I couldn't sleep in bed with her anymore. I slept on the couch near her the first couple nights, until we had a camera hooked up (thanks to our friend, Jeff) so we could see her on a TV screen in our bedroom.

Normal seemed such a distant memory. As we watched the teens walking to our local Jubilee Festival to ride rides and eat fair food, Kevin couldn't help but let his mind wander back to last year. He remembered walking around with Danielle, sharing fried cheese curds. Father's day was hard too; thinking of her usual homemade card and a gift or baked-good she would buy or make especially for her beloved Daddy.

Our town has an unusually early fireworks' display every year. Saturday, June 25th, I was determined to take Danielle to see the fireworks. Kevin wasn't sure if it was a good idea, though she had been having a great day. When he asked Danielle about it, she indicated with her eyes that she wanted to see the fireworks' display. She deserved to get out and experience something special. At 9:30, we loaded her up in the wheelchair and then the van. This always took a great deal of time when trying to work with a Foley Catheter bag and a medicine pump with tubing attached to her chest. When Kevin backed us up to our usual viewing spot, we tucked a blanket around Danielle so the "skeeters" wouldn't get her, leaned her back in her wheelchair, held her head, and enjoyed the fireworks as a family. She actually stayed alert for the first half of the fireworks. It was glorious to take in the fresh air and the beautiful night sky filled with bright bursts of color.

20

Between Heaven and Healing

*T*HE MORNING AFTER, I WOKE up at 6:00 to discover that Danielle had a fever of 104+, labored breathing, a fast heart rate, and a panicked look on her face. How long had she been like that?! Last we checked she was fine. We called home healthcare, which didn't get back with us right away, so we dialed 911. It was determined at Bryan Hospital that she had pneumonia and a urinary tract infection. The fever was not responding at all to medication. She was transported by ambulance to St. V's in Toledo. On the way, her fever spiked to 106.4, even after ice packs were placed around her. She was in obvious distress, as shown by her heart rate. Her fever went down one degree with a rigged-up cooling blanket. Her face looked like it was on fire! I prayed and kept in physical contact with her so she would know I was there. I spoke gently to her, but on the inside I was crumbling. I thought we might not make it to the hospital. I longed to have Kevin by my side. He was following in the van.

We were in good hands at St. V's. The nurses and doctors were extremely thorough in examining Dani. They decided to take her Foley Catheter out for her hospital stay. She hated that contraption, so she was, I'm sure, glad to be free from it for a while. The respirator team began using a vibrating therapy vest to loosen things up in her lungs. Nurses had been suctioning her mouth of phlegm and mucus, as well as suctioning down her nose, too. The nose suction did not look pleasant!

I found myself drawn to snuggling with her in her hospital bed to be close to her and comfort her. Singing to her seemed to calm her heart rate, so I continued to do that often. We also played uplifting Christian music, even at night, since she was awake so much.

Danielle didn't respond to visitors much since she couldn't move anything except her eyes a little. However, when Grandpa Scott came in teasing her, saying "It's good that you get to see me today," we're sure that she was trying to stick her tongue out at him. That was the kind of relationship that Danielle had with her Grandpa Scott, always teasing each other. It encouraged us to see her trying to do something funny.

The day after we arrived at St. V's, Danielle had her first ever seizure. I was in a total panic until the nurse got there. It was not like any seizure I had imagined. She was put on a respirator and sedated. It was a relief to see her at peace. As she was still sleeping that evening, I took my opportunity to sleep in a real bed at the "home away from home" room supplied to us. Kevin and I both went to sleep at 8:00, exhausted. That was the first I had slept through the night since February or early March. Levi was at church camp, oblivious to what was going on. We decided that was a good thing.

We prayed for peace and the next day we arrived in the ICU room to find out our nurse for the day was actually named Peace. That wasn't quite what we had in mind, but proved that God does have a sense of humor. She was a wonderful nurse, as were all the nurses we had there.

Dani's lungs looked good at that point, so it was determined that her brain was not coordinating her breathing. She was also dealing with diarrhea on a daily basis.

My daily routine at St. V's included writing in my journal, reading scriptures and devotions out loud with Danielle, taking at least one walk outside while she napped, and prayer walking in the large chapel. It was good to move, and I could keep my focus on God better while making laps around the chapel. Kevin would join me, if Danielle was sleeping.

> *CaringBridge Journal: July 6, 2011*
> *"Watching her suffer is more than I can bear*
> *This burden is too heavy*
> *Praying for peace and comfort*
> *She's my girl*
> *Didn't know love could be this overwhelming*
> *Didn't know her pain would pierce my heart*
> *so deep*
> *Lord, hear our cry*
> *End this suffering*
> *I know You love her even more than I could*
> *imagine*
> *She's Your child and hand-picked to be ours*

We couldn't ask for a daughter who is more
amazing
She holds our hands and hearts tightly
In the night, when she can't sleep
We find peace in songs to worship You
You encourage us with Your Word
Your promises we cling to with all our being
She's your child, hold her with compassion
Rain down love on her hurting soul
Speak to her softly
Holy Spirit, take control
You are the only one who can know what she
is thinking
The only one she can talk to, since she has no
voice
Give her freedom in You, since her body cannot
move
Help her to be able to sing and dance in Your
presence
To worship You inside her heart"

Eventually, her respirator was replaced with a BiPAP. She was able to be without it during the day, for short periods of time. The tumor was definitely affecting the area that controlled breathing, heart rate, and temperature control, according to an MRI. We were told that she would need to stay on a respirator or a BiPAP permanently.

CaringBridge Journal: July 7, 2011

"Was reminded of a verse today. It is from **Psalm 91. "He who dwells in the secret**

place of the Most High, shall abide under the shadow of the Almighty. I will say of the Lord, He is my refuge and my fortress - my God in Him whom I trust...He will cover you with His feathers and under His wings you will find refuge. His faithfulness will be your shield..." We are resting under His protection and comfort tonight."

We were presented with options at a care meeting on July 12th. We were told that our Danielle was terminal and would need to transition to hospice care. That could mean an in-patient facility or hospice nurses stopping in every day at home. We decided with her breathing difficulties, we would be more comfortable going to an in-patient facility as a transition phase to going home. We would be learning much of her care there, so we could go home, confidently able to care for our daughter. Kevin and I toured the Perrysburg facility that was recommended to us. It would be nice and close for most of our family to visit us, as most of them lived within 20 minutes of there. The doctors and nurses weaned her off some of her meds, only keeping those that would help her to be more comfortable.

Danielle began sleeping more, letting out tiny moans once in a while. Her lips were looking pale. It was so good to see her resting, but at times I became desperate to see those beautiful brown eyes looking at me, even if just for a minute. I lay close to her much of the time, letting the tears flow freely. I sang to her and read to her, not sure if she could hear me, but just in case, I wanted her to have something positive to engage her mind.

There she lay—between heaven and healing.

21

Walking Her Home

O N July 15TH, DANIELLE WAS transported to the Perrysburg Hospice Center. Her room was large and homey with a big picture window facing the pond, flowers, birds, and ducks. We could even open the windows for fresh air and hear the ducks quacking, birds singing, and the relaxing sound of the water fountain. I was able to sleep beside her in a La-Z-Boy. Most of the time we had a steady flow of visitors. In between, we enjoyed the peacefulness of soothing music and the strength that came from constant prayer. Quite a few visitors brought us home-cooked food, flowers from their gardens, or fresh fruit.

The Boulis family was able to all be together for a picnic outside while Danielle slept. It was good to enjoy the outdoors once again.

Whenever nurses came to bathe or change her, I took full advantage of that time to walk around the pond. We tried to have someone in the room at all times with Danielle, while others took breaks to be at the pond or for me to read in the enclosed gazebo. I needed to get away from watching her suffering so I didn't go crazy.

Danielle slept quite a bit. Sometimes her chest would look like she was struggling to breathe, but she was given a medication that would make none of that register in her brain.

Several special visitors came to call. Danielle got a visit from a dog named Toby. She was trying to open her eyes to see him, but with no success. There was also a group of ladies that gathered around Dani's bed and sang several soft, beautiful acapella songs for her.

With the summer sun beckoning on Sunday afternoon, we wheeled Danielle outside to soak up the warm rays of the sun on her skin. It had been 21 days since she had spent time outdoors. We were careful to keep her in the shade most of the time, but we did wheel her bed into the sun for a few minutes and took her sheet off. Levi herded the ducks over to us, so they would quack for her. We basked in the peaceful sound of the water springing up out of the pond and cascading back down. All too soon, it was time to head back indoors. We didn't want to overdo it.

The next morning after our outdoor excursion, the doctor told us that Danielle had begun the process of dying. Her blood pressure was low and her left foot, arm, and hand were cold. It could be hours or up to three days. We prayed once again for a miracle. She hadn't opened her eyes in twenty-four hours. I needed to see her brown eyes, so I actually pried her eyelids open once, just for a second.

Our dear friends, Josh and Toni, had brought Levi home with them to sleep, but after hearing the news, Toni brought him right back up in the morning. Along with Toni was her teenage daughter, who was also a friend of Levi's. Levi leaned on Madison for support that day. We even gave time for her to play guitar for Danielle and for Levi to have time to be with his sister without adults hovering.

Both Toni and Madison were there when a music therapist came to visit that morning. I cannot begin to explain the peace that filled the room as he sang worship songs, accompanied by the gentle sounds of his guitar. The only time he varied from that, was to sing a song from a Disney movie entitled, "A Whole New World."

> "...Unbelievable sights, indescribable feeling
> Soaring, tumbling, freewheeling through an
> endless diamond sky
> A whole new world, don't you dare
> Close your eyes
> A hundred thousand things to see
> Hold your breath— it gets better
> I'm like a shooting star, I've come so far
> I can't go back to where I used to be.
> A whole new world, every turn a surprise
> With new horizons to pursue
> Every moment red-letter..."
>
> (Lyrics by Tim Rice copyright 1992
> Wonderland Music Company)

We all were mesmerized as he sang by Dani's bedside. That song led us to picture Jesus taking Danielle by the hand to show her the wonders of heaven. I thought it was just me, but after talking, we all were thinking the same thing. It was a definite "wow" moment. I couldn't have asked for a better gift on what was to be Danielle's last day with us. Perfect!

22

God Chose Heaven

THAT SAME DAY, JULY 18TH, our entire family came to be with us, except for my brother, Matt, who lives out of state. The nurses had to do some personal care, so everyone was asked to leave the room. I came back soon, alone, wanting to be with her every second while Kevin and Levi sat in the waiting room, surrounded by family and friends.

Crawling into bed with Danielle, I told her that she was the little girl I had wanted my whole life and how proud of her I was and how I enjoyed her creativity, thoughtfulness, and sweet nature. It looked like she was opening her eyes, so I lifted her head to look at me. I couldn't tell if she was looking at me or not. As Danielle did that, she took her last breath. I pleaded with God to raise her up, just like he did for Lazarus, but her body was still. After realizing that it truly was the end, I yelled for Kevin. He couldn't hear me, so I pressed the nurse button and asked her to get him. Meanwhile, I hugged her tight and felt her cheek next to mine. I buried my face in her hair and sobbed. "I'll see you soon, baby," I whispered. Soon would seem like too long for us, but just a moment for her.

I was sure her welcoming committee would include her Great Aunt Evy, Great Uncle Dean, Great Aunt Joyce, her great grandparents that had preceded her in death, and her Aunt Amy's baby that we never got to meet here on earth. I could picture her in her white gown. Dancing. Laughing. Singing. Finally free!

In that moment, Kevin found out the answer to his question of what "OK" meant. Danielle was more than OK; she was perfect in paradise. He remembered the imagery mentioned by a couple people of her dancing in a white gown. Heaven was the answer.

My mind replayed the last few months of Dani's life. She began to have a horrified expression on her face. Her mouth was always open, her hair a mess, her eyes had lost their sparkle. Her limbs had atrophied and had the look of a little elderly lady. All this is what everyone else saw, but when I looked beyond my physical eyes, she had never been so beautiful. Her strength in the Lord and her bravery were her stature. Her faith in God made her face shine like the brightest star. I had never been more proud of her, my daughter, my blessing. She had faced the darkness of death with a light in her soul that even cancer couldn't dim. Danielle trusted her heavenly Father with her very life, and in return she gained access to her eternal paradise a little early.

After the funeral director came for Danielle's body, we packed up the room and drove home. It had been a long while since I had been home. It felt eerie returning without Danielle, though. We would, from here on out, be a family of three.

That night, Gizmo whined at Danielle's door, until we opened it to show him that she was not there. He became our bed buddy and a source of comfort to us. When we would miss Dani, we would call Gizzy over and snuggle with him, burying our faces in his fur. He could handle our tears better than any human.

The next day, we worked steadily to make our house look like a home again, instead of a hospital room. The medical supply company came to take her equipment, and we boxed up and donated the usable leftovers. We wanted to remember Danielle's good days, not her sick ones. Her bedroom had so much equipment in it that her bed had been moved out to be stored at Kevin's parents. We were on a mission to restore her room to look like it was before 2011. It was as if we were erasing the unbearable memories and bringing back the joyful ones. Putting her bed back in place, after all traces of medical paraphernalia were gone, was the final step in making our house look normal again. In my heart, I knew that nothing would be normal again, despite the appearance of normal.

We had decided ahead of time, should she not make it, that we would have her cremated. It seemed foolish for us to spend a pile of money on a casket that would just be buried in dirt and would not be housing her spirit, which had already gone on to heaven. Also, as pastors, we never knew when the next move was, so we didn't want to bury her in a cemetery that we might not even live close to. We wanted to remember Danielle as she looked before cancer ravaged her body, not an image of her lying in a casket with a swollen steroid face and emaciated body.

The "hard" things, like picking up Danielle's ashes and death certificate, did not bring me to tears. The funeral home was wonderful to us! It was the little things that unexpectedly hit me in the gut. As I dropped off Dani's books at the Bryan Middle School, I began crying uncontrollably in the office. It hit me then that she would never again be going to school, and I'd never pick her up for appointments or see her walk down the school hall. A few days later, Mom Boulis brought over a card to sign. I signed Kevin, Melanie, Levi ... and realized that I would never again be signing her name as part of our family. What a sobering thought.

Danielle's memorial service was scheduled for the 31st, so we would have plenty of time to plan. I wanted the whole world to know just how special my daughter was.

Kevin wanted me to pick out a new outfit for the memorial service. Shopping made me think of our Cincinnati trips. I saw a couple Snoopy shirts she would have liked and some purple checkered shoes she definitely would have picked out. I also realized that sitting in hospitals all day and eating away from home had not been kind to my body. Empty-handed, I headed home.

Kevin and I put everything we had in us to prepare for the memorial service. It was after all, the last thing I would do for my girl. There would be no graduation party, wedding to plan, or baby shower. No more birthday parties. As my sister and I put together a photo display for the service, I began to wonder what Danielle would have looked like for her senior picture.

We searched for a copy of Dani singing, "I Can Only Imagine," for her school talent show as a fifth grader. What an interesting choice she had made— a song about heaven. It comforted us to hear her sing about meeting her Lord and Savior face to face. We also found a clip of her reciting Psalm 23 with her kindergarten class. How precious is that!

During our stay at St. V's, I had compiled some Scripture verses and quotes that would be meaningful for Danielle's memorial service, should God choose heaven over healing her here. The ones that popped out at me were:

II Corinthians 4:16-18 "Therefore we do not lose heart. Though outwardly we are wasting away, yet inwardly we are being renewed day by day. For our light and momentary troubles are achieving for us an eternal glory that far outweighs them all. So we fix our eyes not on what is seen, but on what is unseen. For what is seen is temporary, but what is unseen is eternal."

Psalm 116:5 "Precious in the sight of the Lord is the death of his saints."

Due to the large amount of friends and family expected, our church was too small for the service. We were grateful to the large church next door for allowing us to use their sanctuary and building.

At Danielle's memorial service, our family was bursting with pride at hearing the wonderful words spoken about her by teachers, the principal of her school, family, and a couple close friends. The pastor even read a humorous memory, written by Danielle's best friend, Rachel, who was not in attendance due to living in Florida. Hands down, the hardest part of the day for me was walking down the aisle after the service. I couldn't look at anyone, for fear I would see someone else crying and not be able to keep from wailing. It all seemed so real, so final.

23

Picking Up the Pieces

*L*IFE WENT ON, DESPITE MY sorrow. It seemed as if nothing would ever be normal again without Danielle. So many memories—some good, some tormenting. How dare the world keep on spinning when my world had come to a complete stop! How could I be expected to return to life as normal when my heart was in a million pieces, crumbled at my feet?

CaringBridge Journal: August 6, 2011

"One of the hardest things is seeing mothers and daughters together walking down the street or at Wal-Mart. First time I went shopping, it was weird to see life happening normally. It was like I need to say "Don't you know what's happened? I've lost my daughter and there you

all are shopping and checking out as if nothing has happened!"...

...Been really busy! That's probably good. Don't know what I'll do when all of this settles down - when thank-you notes are done, going through Danielle's things, organizing my house, etc. Will feel the void even more then. No one to play games with, bake cookies, walk dogs, or watch "Little House on the Prairie" with, etc. Yes, I know I could find a friend to do those things with, but I don't want to. I want to do them with Dani.

Kevin and Levi have each other. They are similar in so many ways and enjoy doing things together. I'm the odd man out now. I know other people have never had a daughter and feel like you are missing out, but having one for 14 years and now not having her anymore is unbearable. Work seems like just a job to me - used to enjoy it. Everything seems to have lost interest for me. Many have said that I am strong, but I don't want to be strong, I just want to have time to myself for a few weeks more before I have to join in with regular life and pretend that everything is fine. Want to go away on a 2 week vacation somewhere beautiful and do whatever I feel like doing. Wish I could see a glimpse of her in heaven healthier than she's ever been."

CaringBridge Journal: September 22, 2011

"This week and last have been harder on us than the first few weeks. I have had so many tears at such random moments. Kevin has had some rough moments, too. It's hard to forget how much she suffered. Even though she is not suffering anymore, it is hard to get out of our minds. We wish we could have done more for her, spent more time with her, etc. Always wanted to take her horseback riding and was thinking of that recently. Went to the dentist today for a painful experience and remembered the last time I was there was with Danielle when she was starting to have trouble walking. That started a flood of memories. Went to Walgreens and saw lots of Snoopy stuff that she would have loved looking at. That was one of her favorite stores.

I have been in such a weird funk. I have been going through the motions of life, but feel like a zombie sometimes. Having a hard time finding joy in much of anything. Tired a lot and don't want to talk to people as much. Wish I could help others more, but can't seem to get beyond myself right now. Hope all my friends and family will bear with me on this. Don't know how I'll be in the future, but right now I just need to get through life one day at a time. Don't feel so strong anymore. Need to spend more time with God and reading His promises

*and crying out to Him. He has been waking
me up at night to talk to me, since that is when
there are no distractions. I have been convicted
of not having Him first lately. I let the "daily
grind" push Him to the background. So easy
to do, but no excuse.*

*Thanks for all the prayers so many of you have
lifted up for us!"*

In October, Kevin went to a pastor's conference. He shared with me how hard it was being at a hotel without Danielle. Over the course of our travels the last couple years, we had stayed with Danielle in numerous hotels, so his brain automatically connected that experience with Danielle. Even with that, he came back refreshed and ready to jump back into ministry with both feet. I was excited for what God was doing in him and felt like the old Kevin was almost back.

I was asked at the library, by a patron who hadn't seen me in a long time, how Danielle was doing. Tears ran down my cheeks, unashamed, as I expressed that she had passed away. We shared a hug of sorrow, since she had lost her husband within the year. It is amazing how grief can bring people together. I felt especially drawn to people who had experienced the loss of a child. They were the only ones, I felt, who could have any idea of what I was going through. Even people with other losses, I felt could somewhat understand. Not only do situations of a death in the family vary, but reactions vary from person to person.

I have learned that our whole family grieved differently. Levi was doing well, though he preferred not to talk about Dani a lot. I, on the other hand, liked to talk, and loved nothing more than talking about her. That annoyed Levi. His take was that she is so happy now, so why do we need to be sad and wish she were here. He did comment about how strong she was in not complaining much about her sickness and pain. He seemed impressed with her because of that.

I found myself feeling guilty if I could talk about Danielle's death without crying. I also felt equally bad when I cried so easily, as I did most of the time. The world needed to know how much I loved my daughter. I certainly didn't want anyone to think I took her passing lightly. I also wanted the world to know how much strength God had given me and that He truly was helping to comfort me. Feelings are extremely complicated!

CaringBridge Journal: October 9, 2011

> *"Had my first day without tears on Friday and managed another one on Saturday. Some days I miss her so much I don't know how to keep on with life, but days like that make me think I can make it after all. God has such strong arms and I will always love Him and praise Him, even if I don't understand all that had to happen and why she had to suffer and die. If I understood all of it, would that be great faith? This is just a small part of the puzzle of life. I trust God in His great wisdom. I also know that the hard things in life keep me dependent on Him. He cares more about our eternity than about our temporary ease of life."*

Three months without my daughter felt like an eternity. I was feeling the need to keep her memory alive. I just didn't want everyone to forget about her. She was so special to us that I needed her life to matter and have been important.

The library, where I work, was having an oak tree planted in memory of Danielle with an engraving that said, **"I fought the good fight, I finished the race, I kept the faith." II Timothy 4:7**. Perfect! That was how she lived her life.

Whenever I came home to an empty house, I was reminded of Dani's absence. That empty spot on the couch that used to be "her place" was vacant. She had always been genuinely glad to see me come home. Gone was her greeting; replaced by deafening silence. Sometimes I would immediately go curl up in that spot to somehow feel close to her again. Or, I'd go lie on her bed, hug her pillows tight, and let the tears fall.

Reminders of Danielle were everywhere, even beyond our four walls. When I heard "I Can Only Imagine" on the radio driving to church, I got choked up. Then there was the hospital that I passed a few times every week, but out of blue, the sight of it brought a sudden onslaught of memories of when Dani had been there a week in June. When I took the teen girls from our church for a "girl's night out" at the mall, I found myself splitting up from the group for a while. In trying to find an ornament to hang on the Christmas tree in memory of Danielle, I ended up leaving two stores on the verge of a full-blown emotional breakdown.

Many days I tried to drown my sorrow in food or spending money on something that I thought might make me happy. Both of those things brought only fleeting moments of happiness that later brought regret. My only consolation was spending time with God.

24

Living Without Her

*D*ANIELLE HAD NOT ONLY BEEN my daughter, but she had also truly been my best friend. Since we moved often, our family became incredibly close. The first few months of being in a new town full of strangers, we always had each other. Both Dani and I were shy, so making new friends didn't come easily. For me, my life felt too busy to be a good friend, so Danielle just naturally fell into that role in my life. I never tired of spending time with her! She was my game buddy, too. Now I have a cabinet of games and no one to play with.

CaringBridge Journal: November 22, 2011

"So thankful for Danielle getting to be in such a paradise...heaven. Sometimes she didn't always fit in here. She was just herself and wasn't into boys and obsessed with her looks like many girls

her age. She really did love God and was so thoughtful of others most of the time. We all need to remember that we are strangers and aliens in this land and are here for such a short time compared to eternity. Our job is not to fit in, but to make a difference for God. I want to get to heaven and have God be proud of how I lived my life. I know I was proud of how Danielle lived hers.

This week we will have our first holiday without Danielle. I think it will be ok, but I don't know how I'll feel that day.

Can I just say that God is amazing! He has been a source of amazing strength and comfort to me. I never thought I could make it emotionally through something like this. My goal was always being a great mom. My job has never been my source of accomplishment as much as being a great wife and mom was to me. I even felt bad sometimes that I only had two kids - somehow inferior to those with more kids. Now I'm left with just one. I feel bad for Levi that he has no siblings now, but I see God doing some great things in his life recently. I know that God knows what He is doing and can be everything he needs in life.

God can sustain you through anything you go through in life. Even things you think you could never survive. He is totally amazing. Cannot

say thank you enough. Chase after Him now, so
when the storms come, you will have that firm
foundation that will stand through the worst
of storms."

Thanksgiving came and went. Place-cards shaped like leaves were on the table that Danielle had made the year before. Having her handwriting at each place made it feel like she was with us and her memory was alive.

All too soon it was time for Christmas. I seriously considered skipping Christmas, but didn't want to cheat Levi out of anything. He had already lost his sister, so I wanted everything else to be as normal as possible for him. I tried not to mope around too much, crying to myself in my bedroom if I needed to. I wanted to get him an extra-special present, no matter the expense. After all, I only had one child left to buy for. Our family Christmas would forever be changed.

I put up Dani's little tree on our end table and decorated it with all her Snoopy ornaments and the ornaments her Grandma Ann had given her every year as a gift. We also hung a newly acquired ornament with her picture in the middle that reads: "I love you all dearly, now don't shed a tear, I'm spending my Christmas with Jesus this year."

I had snapshots in my mind of last year. Danielle had presented her dad with a coupon book. He only got to redeem one coupon out of it before she got too sick to fulfill all her desires of things to do for her beloved daddy. Then there was the memory of the T-shirt she gave Levi with the gangster Sesame Street characters on it...still his favorite. I wished we had videotaped it all, so we could watch her on that day. I was determined not to put up stockings. Seeing three instead of four would be an everyday reminder of our loss.

I had already gone through Dani's clothes and given most of them away, except for her Snoopy clothes and her Quinceanera dress, but I couldn't bring myself to take her toothbrush out of the holder in the bathroom. How weird was that?

Mid-December Kevin and I attended a memorial service, put on by the funeral home for all the families that had lost loved ones in the last year. I cried through most of it. When her picture popped up during the slide show, I really lost it. It seemed completely wrong to have her picture up there with all the elderly people. For Kevin, having her name in the program was hard. He said her name should have been in a school play program, not in a list of deceased people. It still didn't seem real that she could truly be dead.

I had been praying for a dream of her...a dream that would seem so real that it would be like seeing her alive again. The dream never came.

CaringBridge Journal: December 17, 2011

"Dealing with a little depression and I think Kevin is too. Even Levi is not excited about Christmas this year. I know it is about celebrating Christ and we will still do that, but all else is empty without her. I know we are not alone in this. Many have experienced great loss. Even the loss of a job, a divorce, etc. can make holidays hard for many. If we seem down or uninterested in life right now, it is probably because we are. You may catch us on a good day and we may seem perfectly happy and content and the next day we have a hard time dragging

ourselves out of bed and the house. Just bear with us. We are doing the best we can do right now. We just can't seem to see beyond our own pain sometimes to respond to your needs. We'll get through it, just as I'm sure you all will get through your struggles.

I think all three of us working out 3 times a week has helped us get out some of our stress. Spending time with God is our other lifeline. Both help a lot. Wishing you all a Merry Christmas. Don't forget the birthday boy in all your busyness. He's the reason for all the parties and celebration. Thank you Jesus for coming and saving us from having to pay the consequences of our sin. I, for one, am forgiven and thankful!"

While waiting in line for food at an extended family get-together, I was suddenly overwhelmed with sorrow at the thought of Danielle's absence. I knew she would never again be joining us at any more family get-togethers. Feeling empty and panicked, I had to leave the building for fresh air so I could breathe again. My sobs were carried away by the chilly winter wind. I managed to pull myself together after a few minutes and joined the festivities with a heavy heart.

A few days after that, we heard a knock on the door and opened it to find a stranger holding a couple presents. He just said, "Merry Christmas," and handed them to me. Kevin and I got a gift certificate, and Levi got a cool Aeropostle hoodie and some cologne. The night before, I had been asking God why my little girl couldn't be with me anymore. I think this was His way of saying, "I love you," and am still there for you. I thank God for whoever was obedient to God to bless us in that way.

We all managed to muddle through Christmas parties and events where everyone seemed to have their perfectly complete family surrounding them...that is everyone except us.

CaringBridge Journal: December 29, 2011

"Am glad Christmas is over. It was hard emotionally, especially Christmas Day. The last couple weeks, grief has hit me hard. Haven't shared with many just how much I have been struggling. People always say how strong I am. Now I'm not and that is hard to say. Going through a dry spell spiritually. Not feeling close to God. Going through the motions. Praising God not because I feel like it, but because He is worthy of my praise. Not letting my emotions control me. The weird thing about it is that going through this desert makes me not think about spending time with God - the very thing I need. Going through daily life, sapped of energy - just glad to make it through the day.

Lord, help me to make it through this and bring back my hunger and thirst for Your presence. Give me the ability to minister to others and to want to be around other people. Help me to understand why I had to go through losing my little girl. Help me to trust in Your plan and to not doubt your love and goodness. Fill this

emptiness in my heart with more of you. I need you now, more than ever. Thank you for being my strength up till now. I know that when I am weak, you are strong. I choose to trust you. I know you love Danielle even more than I do. Will you please give me a dream about her in heaven? Love, your daughter and servant, Melanie."

I had been reading books about mourning and thinking about our culture. I am in favor of going back to a physical sign of deep mourning, such as wearing black for a year, as was custom in earlier times. Not that we should walk around sad and somber all the time, but others would understand our fragile emotions if we had an outward sign. When I break into tears at random times, others would know that I am just mourning and would understand. It would seem that the wearing of black clothing would make it acceptable to still be having a hard time and not be expected to just, "get on with life as normal."

Grief can be extremely unpredictable! One day at the library, a sweet young boy was giving the staff a concert in our story-time room. I sat down, thinking how cute he looked. Just a minute into the song, I started tearing up, thinking of Danielle at age nine getting a guitar for her birthday. She loved to play and sing along. I always enjoyed hearing her music. Soon, I was sobbing loud enough to be noticeable and had to leave the room. Even after 15 minutes in the break room, I wasn't able to stop crying. I went back to work, but while I was putting away books all I could think about was how I ached to hear Dani sing and play again. Finally, after an hour of sniffling and weeping, I went home a little early.

Immediately, I searched for something that contained her sweet voice. Finding a DVD of a Christmas play she was in at church, I got to hear her voice as she spoke her lines and sang. How I wish I had her on video playing her guitar!

February brought Valentine's Day and Dani's birthday. I remembered the year before when she sent out Snoopy Valentine cards we had found on clearance the previous year. After she died, I found a few left in her backpack that were never delivered. I had brought them in to school and asked the wonderful secretary to please see that Dani's friends got the cards. We found a valentine Danielle had made for Kevin and me a few years back. She had made a little pocket on the front with three hearts in it. One said, "I love God," the second said, "I love Jesus," and the last said, "I love you, too." She was always so sweet and loved to make us cards and draw us pictures. My mom mailed a picture of Danielle holding her baby cousin Jeannie on her birthday last year. She looked so alive in the picture, still fairly healthy. But seven months ago my baby left this earth. No more pictures. No more birthdays.

25

Hope Springs Anew

*A*FTER THE GLOOMY, FRIGID WINTER of mourning, I felt the Lord warming my heart a bit. Thank the Lord that the joy of spring always eventually comes, even after the bleakest, harshest winters. Throughout the spring, God whispered gentle truths to me and reminders of His love as I tried to carry on with everyday life. It wasn't all a bed of roses, but at least there were flowers in with the ever-present thorns.

CaringBridge Journal: May 8, 2012

"I am amazed how much spring has affected me. The warm sun on my face, the birds singing, the flowers blooming...new life after the bleak, dead, cold winter. My heart has been transformed in a similar manner. I now can see hope where there was not much before. I still have my days

(ask Kevin), but hope is springing up, like a new plant breaking through the hard, stony soil. A couple months ago, I was convinced that I needed counseling to get through this. It just wasn't getting any better and I was trying to muddle through the acts of life, but very dead inside. I am thankful for Christian counselors, but this time God wanted it to be just Him and me.

Am finding working outside very therapeutic. Never was one to love gardening like some people, but I do now. It's a great time of quiet for me to talk to God and listen to Him speak to me. As I planted seeds, I was totally amazed that those tiny seeds will soon become nourishing veggies for my family, expanding in size by miraculous amounts. Isn't God amazing to plan all that! It's the same in our lives. When we are obedient to do what He asks of us, He can take it and turn it into something much greater. If we keep it, it's just a tiny, little thing, but when we let Him water it and shine His glory on it, it can grow into something amazing. The Bible says that He gives us all a measure of faith and that with the faith of a mustard seed we can move mountains. Imagine what He can do with a seed as big as a bean seed (that was by far the biggest seed I planted in my garden). I am making a daily decision to die to myself and submit to Christ and am expecting Him to use my life to bear much fruit. (The fruit of the Spirit

is love, joy, peace, patience, kindness, goodness,
faithfulness, gentleness and self-control.) Some
of these fruit are pretty puny right now in my
life, but with God as the Gardner of my life, I'm
expecting a great harvest!"

Despite there being more good days than bad days by then, I found my mind wandering back to the dark days of those last few months of Dani's life. It was (and still is) a daily choice for me to dwell on where she is now instead of her days of suffering. During those times I may not have seen Him working in her, but I know God's heart. I believe He was holding her hand and being her strength when all her strength was gone.

During the month of May, I decided to get on Danielle's Facebook page and read some of her posts. I typed in her name and no results came up. In a full panic, I tried again and thought her account was deleted. I desperately needed to read her thoughts and words at that moment to feel close to her. I then realized that all I had to do was read through my friend list and click on Dani's name there. Whew—what a relief when her "wall" popped up. As I started to read, I became obsessed with reading every one of her entries all the way back to when she first started Facebook. Some entries made me laugh; some made my eyes fill with tears. Since she is not with me physically, her words seemed priceless to me. After my scare, I decided to print off all her Facebook comments, just in case they were ever deleted. Dragging myself to bed late, I fell asleep thinking of my Danielle during the good days.

The next morning it hit me. BAM! Do I treat God's word as that precious? Am I obsessed with reading His words? He should be more important to me than Danielle. His words in the Bible are how He most often speaks to us. Am I willing to stay up late or get up early to read His words? I must admit, sometimes the answer is no. His words are a treasure, and I hope I remember that every day.

Mother's Day went well. Someone must have been fervently praying for me! I missed Danielle's usual handmade card. She hadn't made one the year before, either. The last thing she had made for me was the "I (heart) MOM" picture from our time in Texas. I had it framed so I could see it often and be reminded of her thoughtfulness. To take the focus off myself and my feelings, I had invited Kevin's family over for a barbeque lunch. A rosebush was presented to me by my in-laws as a new addition for the flower garden we were making in memory of Danielle. Later, to fulfill my wish, Levi and Kevin played a game of Skip-Bo with me. Danielle and I had played that game often, especially when both of us were itching to play games, but couldn't convince the guys to join in on a game with us. To top the day off, Levi and I spent some much needed bonding time making homemade soft pretzels that would rival any fresh, hot pretzel I've ever tasted. At the close of the day, I asked God to do some favors for me: "give Danielle an extra big hug from me, and take care of my little girl."

His reply was, "You know I always do. She is so happy here. She has no pain. She has no fear, and she loves all the animals here. I love you, Melanie."

"I love you too."

Kevin and Levi had been training to run a 5K together since last September. I started out training with them too, but due to my hips constantly going out of place and many trips to the chiropractor, I had to stop training after only a few months. I still took walks and tried to keep in shape, but was limited to what I could do. Exercising was a great stress release for all of us. Just a couple weeks before the Memorial Day 5K, I was finally able to start running again, but it was too late to work my way up to that kind of distance.

CaringBridge Journal: May 29, 2012

"Yesterday was the 5K we were supposed to run as a family. We just needed to do something that made our family feel complete. I am still bummed that I didn't get to run with the guys. Felt like the odd man out. Honestly, I had some conversations with God when my hip was constantly going out of place that were filled with frustration. As if God owed us a perfect year of health since we had already gone through so much. I know that is not the most rational thought, but I thought it all the time. It has been anything but great health for me. The guys have been pretty healthy, though.

So…yesterday morning I didn't even want to go to the race. Before it started, I was feeling pretty down and had moments of trying to hold back tears. Those of you who know how easily I cry will be amazed to know that I made it through without crying! It was supposed to be a family thing for all three of us. Definitely feeling Danielle's absence the last few days.

My faith has been tested more in the last couple years than in my whole life combined, I think. God has provided for us financially many times, so that wasn't a huge concern, but in other areas, I haven't had to deal with before. I still struggle with the "whys", knowing I may never know the answer. I still struggle with God not healing her of her tumor on this earth. Some people following her story, I felt like, could have witnessed that miracle and been a turnaround in their lives to see God's awesome power work through a healing miracle. Some don't even believe in God, or were questioning if they really want to follow Him. I am thinking "How can Dani dying bring more glory to God and do more for His kingdom than doing a healing miracle would have?" Just when I think I'm OK with not knowing why and trusting in His goodness and the big picture that I cannot see, I start down that rabbit trail again.

My human-ness has reared its ugly head more lately and reminded me how anything good I am is because of Jesus, not because I'm a nice person naturally. Gotten critical, judgmental, etc. and not proud of it. Can I just take a vacation from life now, please!!!! Vaca time is coming soon, but not soon enough. I pray

*that the week will not go too quickly. Kevin
and I both want it to double as a spiritual
retreat and take lots of time to seek God for
direction in our lives. I have started this week
getting up early. Trying to get in a routine of
doing that so I can exercise and spend more
time with God in the morning. Trying to get
out of my spiritual rut. We are all as close to
God as we want to be. If we want to be closer,
it comes with sacrifice. More time seeking
Him, reading His Word, listening to Him,
putting Him first (even above your family).
Am positive that God will not bless my life if I
am at all lukewarm. Need to stay passionate
for Him!"*

In early June, we finally had the opportunity to get away
from our daily schedules and travel to the Outer Banks of
North Carolina. Three of Kevin's cousins and their families
joined us. Since we were with a group, we didn't feel Danielle's
absence every moment, like we would have felt if it was just
the three of us. We had lots of laughter, games, sun, good food,
and time with God. I spent my 39th birthday at our beach
house. That day I was choked up thinking about Levi now
being an only child. When we got in vehicles, Levi was the
only kid that didn't have a sibling to ride with. He rode with
cousin Joe's family to the shops we went to that day while I
cried on the way there. Family get-togethers will be so small.
I think of my parents and their siblings and all the kids and
how much fun it is for the big group. It will just be us with Levi
and his wife and kids someday. I'm hoping and praying that

he marries a wife with siblings that he gets along with well to have that family feel.

Along our drive home, we stopped in Luray, Virginia, to visit some caverns. We were commenting on how Danielle would have loved seeing the beauty of the stalactites. I then thought about all the cool sights there must be in heaven and how it wouldn't compare to the caverns anyway. I can't wait to see how beautiful and breathtaking heaven must be!

26

Trust and Obey

*I*T'S BEEN A YEAR NOW since I've seen my daughter. The moments of living in a dream-world, where it seems she might walk in the door at any time, have passed. Her death seems final now. I still have a hard time watching mothers and daughters have their special moments that I will never get to share with Danielle. Every baby shower reminds me that I will not get the chance to see Danielle enter the awesome world of motherhood. Every graduation party is a reminder that I will never see her walk across the stage and receive her diploma as I proudly clap and beam in the stands. (I thought of her memorial service as her graduation into heaven, though.) Every school musical reminds me that Danielle was just one year away from experiencing the hard work and joy that being a cast member would have brought her. We'll never scrapbook together, sing duets, bake cookies, or shop for Christmas presents again. I realize that she is not missing any of these things and that heaven is grander than all of these experiences combined. But until I get to heaven, I am afraid that I will be missing Danielle and all the "what ifs" we could have experienced together had she lived. She definitely got the better end of the deal in our separation.

Longing for heaven most days, I plod along on this earth, realizing that God has plans for my life and I need to live in the here and now to accomplish His will. I need my life to matter. Dreams I had put on hold, I am now chasing as the Lord's timing allows. Seeking Him daily is the only way to know what dreams I am to pursue. Some are just my own wants and some are God-given dreams.

I pray that I might be a blessing to others who are experiencing deep grief or those asking God, "Why?" because of prayers not answered in the way they expected. My constant awareness of heaven serves me well in remembering why I'm here. My goal is to bring as many people to heaven with me as I can. It seems I can reach people through writing and music better than any other way, so that is what I am concentrating on. Each of us is unique in our God-given personalities. I will influence people some could never reach, and others can touch lives that I never could.

Faith is easy, until God asks for something difficult of me. Even in writing this book I have stepped out in faith! When I walk in obedience, He trusts me with more responsibility and seems to then ask me to take gigantic leaps of faith. These leaps can lead to huge victories for the Kingdom of God, as overwhelming as they may seem in the beginning stages. I have always heard, but am now seeing in action, that the worst kind of failure is doing nothing out of fear of failing. If God is for us, who can be against us? I know we wrestle against the powers of Satan, who is constantly seeking lives to ruin, but God's strength in us can always bring victory.

I want to see miracles, but I don't like being in a situation that necessitates one. God may never part the water in my life because my feet are planted on dry ground. I wait for God to move when God is saying to me, "Get your feet wet." If I make a move, I'll see God move. Trusting in His answer and how He might move in my situation is the tough part. **Isaiah 55:8-9** says, **"For my thoughts are not your thoughts, neither are your ways my ways, says the LORD. For as the heavens are higher than the earth, so are my ways higher than your ways, and my thoughts than your thoughts."**

Sometimes God allows my small plans to fail so that His big dream for me can succeed. The question is, do I trust Him?

27

Praising Him In The Storm

I HAVE LEARNED THAT HEAVEN IS healing. I can't always comprehend why God does things the way He does, but I do know that He is love. Throughout my life, He has been a faithful God and has come through time and time again. Sometimes, when my prayers are not answered the way I think they should be, later on, I understand why. Danielle going to heaven instead of being healed on earth is one of those "whys" I may not know until I enter eternity myself.

As an inquisitive, sometimes impatient person, I have trouble with not knowing. That's where faith steps in. I found a Bible verse that even addresses this thought. **Isaiah 57:1-2 says: "The righteous perish, and no one takes it to heart; the devout are taken away, and no one understands that the righteous are taken away to be spared from evil. Those who walk uprightly enter into peace; they find rest as they lie in death."** When I think about that, why would I think my loving heavenly Father wouldn't want the best for my daughter? Heaven IS the best. He wasn't being evil and cruel when He took her from this earth; He was doing the most loving thing possible. This world is becoming more evil all the time. We have to live in it right now, but Danielle was spared having to experience any further the heartaches that this world has to offer. This world is not our home; it is just a temporary life. We long for a better life sometimes. That better life is out there—it is eternity with God in heaven. Only God knows best when to call us home.

I have a choice to make every day. Am I going to be mad at God because I don't get to be with Danielle right now, or do I choose to love Him and praise Him in the hard times? I think of Job, who went through more suffering than any human being that I know of. After finding out that all of his oxen, donkeys, sheep, servants, camels, and children were dead, we are told: **"At this, Job got up and tore his robe and shaved his head. Then he fell to the ground in worship and said: 'Naked I came from my mother's womb, and naked I will depart. The LORD gave and the LORD has taken away; may the name of the LORD be praised'."** (**Job 1:21-21**) Wow!

Between heaven and healing. From March 2009 through July 2011, my whole heart and soul was desperate for healing for Danielle. I longed for nothing else. I prayed for nothing else. I knew until she breathed her last breath that restoring Danielle to full health was totally possible for the Creator's Hands. My God is Great, full of mercy, and compassionate. Through it all, I clung to His promise that He would never leave me nor forsake me. Now, more than ever, I cling to His promise that, "Whosoever believes in Him shall not perish, but have everlasting life." I am so glad that my dear Danielle made her choice to love God and to trust Him with her life, even in the face of death. Heaven and hell are a reality. I would like to think that her death caused many to think about their eternities and in turn, make a decision to follow Christ Jesus. My anchor in this life is Jesus Christ. My confidence in life eternal is in His finished work at the cross. Danielle Louise Boulis. My daughter. Heaven: July 18, 2011. This mother's journey. My heart is at peace.

Epilogue

While I do know that God heals people in amazing ways this side of heaven, I have seen several examples in my own life of Godly men and women who weren't healed here on earth. They are not second-class citizens who failed the class on faith. These are people who trusted and loved God, even while staring death in the face. God was their strength until the very end, even when their strength was gone. God was able to give them peace and joy despite their circumstances. Those are miracles indeed! I don't understand why God heals one and not another. I'll never understand. Do I love Him only when He does things exactly how I was hoping? As a parent, I have a goal in mind of what I want my child to grow up to be, and I make decisions that will support building those characteristics in him. Do I not think that my Father knows best? God has a specific plan for each one of us, and He allows things that will build the kind of character we need to fulfill the mission He has for us.

Many say, "God never gives us more than we can handle." The verse they are referring to is so often misquoted. I Corinthians 10:12-13 says, in referring to temptations or testing, " So, if you think you are standing firm, be careful that you don't fall! No temptation has overtaken you except what is common to mankind. And God is faithful; he will not let you be tempted beyond what you can bear. But when you are tempted, he will also provide a way out so that you can endure it." Outside of temptation, I think God regularly gives us more than we can handle so that we will need to rely on Him. I have seen this played out in my life and the lives of many I know. If my life seems "out of control," that could be God's way of turning my focus back on Him—letting me know that in this life I desperately need to lean on Him, and for me to be aware that I have no power on my own. Any strength that I have comes from God.

Isaiah 40:28-31 says: "Do you not know? Have you not heard? The LORD is the everlasting God, the Creator of the ends of the earth. He will not grow tired or weary, and his understanding no one can fathom. He gives strength to the weary and increases the power of the weak. Even youths grow tired and weary, and young men stumble and fall; but those who hope in the LORD will renew their strength. They will soar on wings like eagles; they will run and not grow weary, they will walk and not be faint."

As I read the Bible, especially the Old Testament, God did some things I find to be extremely harsh. In my human reasoning, some of His decisions don't seem fair. God's sense of justice doesn't have to fit my reasoning. He is God. God's sense of justice is definitely higher than my thinking can fathom.

Most days I feel like praising God, but sometimes it is a sacrifice to praise Him. On those days that I don't especially feel like praising Him, I make that decision to still proclaim His greatness. Once I begin to, I am filled with love to back up the words I am singing or saying. It's a lot like marriage. Some days I feel "in love" with my spouse, with lots of warm fuzzies. Other days, even though I always love Kevin, I don't feel anything. I choose to act loving and respectful despite the lack of feelings. Those feelings eventually catch up to my actions. Love is a choice, not a feeling. Worship and praise to our God is also a choice. As I praise Him through the storms, my relationship with Him deepens and I feel love for Him once again, in time.

My prayer is that if this finds you in the storms of life, that you remember that God is still there, above the storm clouds that block our view. He is still in control. God sometimes calms the storms. Other times, He holds our hand and puts His arm around us as we keep walking—despite the pounding rain and the wind that threatens to knock us down flat. When we can't see His hand, we must trust His heart. I pray that you will know the depths of His love for you, and that even though life is hard—God is faithful. Until that day, when those who love and follow God enter into paradise, we will face the storms of life. Hold onto the God who is able to carry you through. You were never meant to face life alone, without Him.

About the Boulis'

Melanie Boulis is a librarian. She is active at her church leading worship, working with the food pantry ministry, and teaching a class on Wednesday nights. Melanie also enjoys reading, baking, scrapbooking, playing piano, and singing. She hopes to learn how to play Danielle's guitar in the near future.

Kevin Boulis is the pastor of First Assembly of God in Bryan, Ohio, and works part-time at the library. He graduated from Central Bible College in Springfield, Missouri, with a degree in Youth Ministry and Biblical Studies. Kevin enjoys playing basketball, football, golfing, and is a huge fan of Cleveland sports. You can listen to Kevin's weekly sermons at: bryanfirst.org.

Levi Boulis attends Bryan High School and will graduate in 2013. He plans to be a youth pastor and is taking classes with Global University toward that goal. Levi is also an artist, mostly drawing with charcoal. He throws discus and shot put on his track team, enjoys running, and is a sports fan, like his dad. Levi is also involved in his church youth group.

Suggested reading:

Confessions of a Grieving Christian by Zig Ziglar

The Boy Who Came Back From Heaven: A Remarkable Account of Miracles, Angels and Life Beyond This World by Kevin and Alex Malarkey

A Place of Healing: Wrestling with the Mysteries of Suffering, Pain, and God's Sovereignty by Joni Eareckson Tada

Choosing to SEE: A Journey of Struggle and Hope by Mary Beth Chapman

An Early Journey Home: Helping Families Work Through the Loss of a Child by Mary Ann Froehlick

I Still Believe by Jeremy Camp

Heaven Is For Real by Todd Burpo

Heaven by Randy Alcorn

The Thrill of Victory– the Agony of Defeat by Randy Clark

Suggested Music:

Beauty Will Rise CD by Steven Curtis Chapman

You Deliver Me CD by Selah

Stay CD by Jeremy Camp

"With hope" by Steven Curtis Chapman on CD Speechless

"Homesick" by MercyMe on CD Undone

"Save a Place For Me" by Matthew West on Something to Say CD

"I Can Only Imagine" by MercyMe on CD Almost There

"Held" by Natalie Grant on CD Awaken

"Praise You In This Storm" by Casting Crowns on Lifesong CD

"Yet I will Praise You" by Andy Park on CD In the Secret

"Face to Face" by Stephanie Staples on CD Face to Face

CPSIA information can be obtained at www.ICGtesting.com
Printed in the USA
BVOW072028170113

310940BV00001B/1/P